REAL ESTATE STORIES

Gonzo Management

To Amos,

Write more

Books.

TJ Lars

REAL ESTATE STORIES

Gonzo Management

**Hilarious & Uncensored Tales
From A Property Management Expert**

TERRY KASS

Real Estate Stories: Gonzo Management
Hilarious & Uncensored Tales From A
Property Management Expert

Published by:
Greater Phoenix Commercial Investments, Inc.
www.gpci-az.com

ISBN: 978-0615919102

To Mike and Mike:

The first got me into the business.

The second kept me in the business.

I will always appreciate your confidence in me,

and so help me if it takes forever, I will

get you both back.

TABLE OF CONTENTS

INTRODUCTION

There are many ways to make a living.

You could drive trucks. You could answer phones. You could serve coffee. You could tap dance in front of an upturned hat and hope for the best. The career possibilities are virtually limitless.

I chose a career in real estate, and if you're holding this book, you probably have too, are curious about the profession, or in need of a good laugh.

In any case, when you think of a person who works in real estate you might envision a sharp-dressed Realtor® sitting on a park bench or in a television commercial waiting to sell your home. You may be envisioning the person who hosted tours and arranged furniture and printed out flyers to sell your home, or the person who gave you a tour of a well-arranged home you'd seen on a flyer before you bought your home. You might even think about the person who owns the apartment building you live in and gold-plates his mansion with your rent payments.

You probably aren't thinking about the property manager. What the profession lacks in glamor and notoriety, it makes up for in money, opportunity, and sheer entertainment value.

In fact, you may not really know what a property manager does. What's involved in managing a property? You probably know that they occasionally turn up at a tenant's door, but what are they there for? Do they collect rent from reluctant tenants? Ferret out illegal activities? Combat armies of termites and cockroaches? Intervene in the lives of hopeless hoarders on the brink of eviction? Pet sweet, loving Pit Bulls and outwit drug dealers?

If you pursue a career in property management, you'll be doing all of the above and much more. There's no need to panic – whether you've already started down the road to property management greatness, or are considering dipping your toe in real estate, this book will tell you everything you need to know to be successful, calm, prepared, brave, and more attractive to the opposite sex. "Real Estate Stories" will give you an insider's look into the zany world of property management. And you'll enjoy some good belly laughs along the way, too!

As a property manager, it'll be your job to open doors. Now, let me tell you what's behind them.

CHAPTER ONE

You Have How Much?

Quick, think of something that sounds like more fun than property management. What did you come up with? Knee surgery, root canals, ingrown toenails, and passing a kidney stone are all acceptable answers. You might also have come up with fun-filled activities like getting mauled by a bear, visiting your mother-in-law's, and slamming your hand in a car door. It's the sort of thing that only a complete and utter lunatic would enjoy. And yet, despite that, hundreds of thousands of seemingly-normal people jump into the fray of real estate investment and management each and every year.

So why do they do it?

In a word: money. With a little bit of luck, skill and perseverance, a career in real estate is the best way there is to make money. There are more millionaires made through real estate than any other type of investment; at least, there are if you believe my dad. Is my dad an internationally recognized authority on real estate investment returns? Absolutely not. Was he the man who helped me launch my own real estate career? Of course he was, and I knew I had a much better chance of getting him to cooperate if I listened to every word he said. Looking back, it's hard to tell what helped me more – his words of wisdom, or the fifty thousand dollars he loaned me to get started.

Probably the money, but I won't tell him that.

I didn't always have dreams of being a high-rolling, glamorous real estate mogul. Once upon a time, I was nothing more than a humble winery worker at the Chateau St. Jean Winery in Sonoma, California. In place of tenants and inspections, my days were filled with Chardonnays and Cabernets. Then one day, while wandering between the bottle racks, it suddenly dawned on me that I wanted to be a millionaire.

There were only two problems with my newfound ambition. For one, it's very difficult to become a millionaire by working in a winery. As it turns out, the ability to memorize long lists of wines of various quality (try a Chateau Lafite Rothschild, if you ever get the chance) does not warrant nearly the kind of financial compensation it deserves. So I looked towards real estate, and that was where my second problem emerged – I knew absolutely nothing about it. Sure, I'd bought houses to live in, and at some point I'd briefly dealt with the people who sold those houses, but that was where my real estate experience ended. I was roughly as prepared for a career in property management as I was for a career as a kangaroo farmer. I wouldn't know a good deal if it came up and kicked me in the face.

So why do it?

There's a saying that goes a little something like "big risks create big returns", and nowhere is that more true than real estate. Buying property is no small matter; unless you have enough cash to fill an Olympic-sized swimming pool you can't just casually purchase some building that catches your eye when you're out on your next coffee run. Luckily, it's a risk that pays off. There are lots of ways to invest large sums of money: you could blindly dump it into a shady offshore investment, start up a cheese factory, or buy up as many shares in tambourine manufacturing stock as you can find – but real estate is the best choice. You own a reliably appreciating asset. And look on the bright side – even in a total economic crash, that house you bought is going to make a much better shelter than a pile of worthless stock certificates.

Oh, and it wasn't just the prospect stable investments and sure-fire homelessness contingency plans that drew me into real estate. There was another teensy, tiny reason for my attraction to the field. You see, my younger brother invests in real estate.

As does my other brother.

And my dad.

And my uncle.

And my mother's cousin.

In fact, everyone but the family cat seems to have their hand in the real estate cookie jar. Only one of my family members actually hit the elusive seven-figure mark – one of my younger brothers – but the rest were able to make enough money to pay for their own homes and allow themselves the comfort of knowing they'll never be forced to subsist on packaged ramen.

I wanted in. And the fifty thousand dollars ($50,000) from my father was my ticket (Side note – in real estate contracts, always express amounts both words and numerals. This hint alone is worth the price of the book). It was the year 1993, and for those of you too young to remember it (or perhaps too old to remember much of anything), it was the final year of the worst real estate market the United States had ever seen. Everything that could have gone wrong, did go wrong – between the IRS tax change in 1985, bankrupt savings and loans, and massive real estate losses, a career in real estate seemed roughly as promising as a career in shark taming.

By pure, dumb luck, I'd chosen to start my career in the best possible year to buy.

Now, I could have said that this fortuitous decision was the result of extensive research into the market, talking to seasoned pros, evaluating charts, graphs, trends, income statements, and a very promising reading from a physic hotline. In reality, I spent most of that period of my life glued to reruns of Gilligan's Island (I had a huge crush on Mary Anne) with a glass of Chardonnay in hand. The timing was little more than a happy cosmic accident.

Cosmic accidents, however, are very difficult to replicate, and the fifteen years of my career that followed the 1993 season had less to do with luck and more to do with patience and rigorous application of common sense. It all started with my first building.

How do you purchase your first real estate investment not knowing the first thing about the subject? You could check the newspaper for available income property, or trust the decision to a real estate salesperson. In my case, we started with the paper and ended up using the salesperson. Now, at the time, I didn't know anything about investing in multi-family housing (an endearing term for buildings that most humans know as apartments), but I did hold an MBA with an advanced degree in business. I figured I must be able to analyze an investment for its viability - cash flow, vacancy history, condition of building, presence of alligators in the toilets, and return on investment. And I've spent enough time living in houses to look for obvious signs of trouble, like termite damage or missing roofs.

For instance, I knew, even then, to look for properties near the area I was living in. That advice holds true to this day – if you have any plans to self-manage, buying nearby properties is a must. Gas costs about as much as unicorn blood, and living near your work will save you a lot of time and money on commuting as well as fear and anxiety from venturing into unknown territory. Also, if you deem an area to be suitable and relatively bear-free enough to live in, chances are – if you have good taste – other people might enjoy living there as well. There is, however, something to be said about purchasing investment real estate in the "challenging" areas. Your life becomes more exciting; the criminals and drug dealers are shockingly reliable with rent payments, and you even get to become best friends with the local law enforcement personnel. Starting a Batman-calibre safety regime is a good idea if you're tempted by sketchy neighborhoods: take the concealed weapons class, learn martial arts, have a good health plan, stay away at night, and develop a healthy distrust of your fellow man; it might come in handy.

Unfortunately, "stay close to home" wasn't quite enough advice to get me through my first deal. You might think that my property-mogul family told me exactly what to do then. I did reach out to them, but there was one little problem – they all lived in Chicago, and I was in Phoenix. They gave me general advice about the types of areas to look in, current investment returns, structural issues, and how to tell if my tenants might be drug-dealing axe murderers, but success in real estate is mostly based on that old adage, "location, location, location", and therein lay the problem. They knew nothing about the real estate market in Phoenix.

I was on my own.

But I didn't panic. I looked in the local newspaper, drove around the immediate area, and started coming up with possible investment opportunities. I called the owners or realtors, and set up appointments to see properties. At that point, I was mostly interested in four-plexes. With fifty thousand dollars ($50,000) nestled in my sweaty palms, I figured I had enough money to put down a 30% down payment and, like everyone else in the world who isn't sitting on a vast empire of wealth, get a loan for the remaining balance.

How do I properly explain what it's like walking into investment real estate with no knowledge, experience, or education? Picture this: you're driving down a secluded highway surrounded by big trees on both sides. You're going about 70 miles per hour, it's night, and you're almost falling asleep, because driving down secluded highways at night is boring, and you've been driving for hours. All of a sudden, a deer walks into the middle of the road and turns its head towards you; the eyes light up red, and there's nothing you can do. You're going to hit it.

I'm the deer.

Every time I walked into a complex, I would freeze with my eyes wide open, ready to bolt; I had no idea what I was doing. It started to get old, four-plex after four-plex. Eventually, I was so fed up with the whole process that I'd just about made up my mind to drink myself into a coma, pack up my things, move off to Sante Fe and try my hand at opening a Mexican restaurant. I'd already gotten started on the drunken coma part of my plan with a bottle of Pinot Noir (Dry, great fruit, soft, one of my favorite types), when the phone rang – it was my best friend Mike on the other end. It wasn't an intervention, as I'd feared.

It was the most important phone call in my investment career.

We were making the usual small talk – women, sports, delicate fine wines – when he happened to mention that he was thinking of investing in the very same Phoenix real estate market that I was struggling in. Mike wasn't just some disgruntled garbage man with a pipe dream – he was a Certified Public Accountant, running his own environmental clean-up business. I didn't have any oil spills to mop up, but he did have skills I needed – he could analyze cash flow, take care of financial paperwork, and read through endless piles of dull tax information. Still, at the time, he lived in an apartment in the South Chicago area, drove a 1985 Dodge, had a lovely wife, and in my mind, was the last guy I would be talking to about investing in Phoenix real estate. I'd never so much as seen the man break the speed limit; I hadn't pegged him as the 'risk-taker' type.

Still, out of curiosity, I asked him how much money he had to invest.

He told me he had one million dollars.

Naturally, I didn't believe him. I couldn't believe that any friend of mine had that kind of money on hand, let alone a friend who drove a used car and had a kitchen so small you had to suck in your stomach to get through the door. But he insisted he was telling the truth, and once my dizziness and heart palpitations had subsided, I knew we were in business. $50,000 is the domain of rank amateurs. One million dollars was enough to make serious investors sit up and pay attention.

We were in the big leagues.

Since this is supposed to be a humorous look at the world of property management, I'll spare you the long and hideously boring details of my first purchase. I will tell you that we bought a 44 unit apartment complex from the Resolution Trust Company (Real Estate liquidation arm of the United States government), and we paid with a briefcase full of cash, like Hollywood mobsters. We got a smoking deal, and my property management career caught fire. Mike supplied the cash and I supplied the time, energy, stress, headaches, heartburn, panic-induced hallucinations, and put my life in danger (well, sometimes) managing our soon-to-be growing apartment empire.

And that's where the fun began.

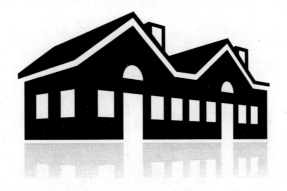

CHAPTER TWO

Drug Dealers 101

Drugs are usually no laughing matter. If you announce to your family that you've taken up using heroine, you probably won't expect them to greet the news with loving smiles. Drug dealers cause all kinds of problems – for families, police forces, and apartment managers, among others – but every now and then, one of them does something so incredible that it can only be described as "amazing, but true". Over the course of my career, I've dealt with every kind of controlled substance peddler, from the extremely dangerous to the unintentionally hilarious. When I first started out, I didn't have a guide to dealing with drug dealers; if a career in property management is in your future, be sure to pay close attention to this chapter. It'll save you a lot of time, money and heartache, and it might even give you a few great stories to bring home to the dinner table.

Now, before you can begin to collect your own tales of drug dealer run-ins, you need to learn how to spot your prey. Luckily, the elusive drug dealer is not a subtle creature; it leaves plenty of clues in its wake.

The first thing you'll notice is an apartment that gets a lot of visitors. Not just any visitors, mind you. These are the types of visitors that show up at all hours of the day and night, stay for a minute or three, and go off on their merry way again. It might look like your tenant is loaning cups of sugar to the entire neighbourhood, but chances are, those people are showing up in search of a very different white powder.

The next thing that will become very apparent are the parties. Drug dealers don't just invite a few friends over for drinks on Friday nights – they throw house-trashing, brain-cell-smashing raves that last all through the night, every single night of the week. The party's guests never seem to go home, either; they simply hole up like bats during the daylight, and start the party all over again the moment the sun sets.

Another thing that might raise an eyebrow is a tenant who only pays his rent in cash – sometimes with a little extra. The only people who routinely have that much cash on hand are wait staff, strippers, and drug dealers, and even the former two tend to keep their money in bank accounts. Finding a little bonus added to the rent payment is also cause for alarm – the tenant may be trying to buy your silence in small, unmarked bills.

If you manage to ignore these signs and you let your drug dealer problem get seriously out of hand, you might actually notice police beginning to monitor the occupants of the apartment in question. Keep an eye out for unusual glints of light coming from windows in nearby buildings – you might just be seeing the sun's reflection off the lens of a police telescope.

By far the most obvious sign of a drug dealer, however, beyond parties or rent payments or police, is a good look at the drug dealer himself. Should you actually manage to get a good look at one in sunlight, you'll notice that they look like bulbous, emaciated aliens, or cute little drugged E.T.s.

So what do you do when you realize that a drug dealer is renting one of your units?

That's when the fun really begins.

The first thing you should always do is sit down with your drug dealer, and engage him or her in a long, intellectual discussion. Point out the harm that drug dealing does to society, and back up your statements with concrete examples and relevant statistics. If possible, provide the dealer with several pamphlets for drug rehabilitation centres – they love those. It may take a little work, but the drug dealer will confess the error of his ways, thank you for putting his life back on track, and make immediate plans to move out.

Just kidding. He's going to deny every word you say.

But let's back up for a minute. Confronting a drug dealer actually goes a little something like this:

You've noticed all the signs – the constant foot traffic, the non-stop parties and the increased police activity. The unit perpetually resembles the Mos Eisley cantina from Star Wars. It's time to take action. So you walk up to the unit, knock on the door, pray to every God you've ever heard of that no one answers, and you wait. You're quite familiar with the sleep cycle of the domestic drug dealer by now, and you know that since it's 2:00pm on a weekday you've got a pretty good chance of catching them at home. If you really want to coax them out, you could even try dressing up as one of their customers; put on dirty clothes, muss your hair, stop shaving and showering – be creative.

When your well-groomed, law-abiding young tenant – I mean, scruffy, delinquent, drug dealer – answers the door, introduce yourself as the manager of the building. It might seem absurd to have to introduce yourself to someone who already met you when you rented them the unit, but you have to remember that this man – or woman, I'm not prejudiced – is high most of the time. Odds are, they spend so much time immersed in a haze of Technicolor dragons and flying hot dogs that they wouldn't recognize their own mother. Really emphasize that you're not one of their usual customers, and look for any kind of glimmer of recognition in their eyes.

Once you've discerned that your tenant is mostly coherent, present your case about the tenant's suspect trafficking. He (or she) will look at you like you've got three heads and a broccoli plant growing out of your ear. The denials will start off calm, and gradually crescendo to a tidal wave of unintelligible hysterics. You might start to feel hysterical yourself at that point, but it's important to keep your temper in check. Walk away. Take a few deep breaths. Play a round of Angry Birds on your phone. Take a swig of whatever calming elixir you keep in your hip flask. Then serve the tenant an immediate eviction notice.

Now, that scenario might sound more like a lifetime movie than a comedy, but some of the funniest moments of my career came from confrontations with drug dealers. My all-time favorite drug story took place in a 104-unit building that I purchased directly from an insurance company for a little more than a song. How did I get such a smoking deal on the building? It was easy – I used my good looks, charm, wit and winning smile to drive the cost down.

Oh, and the building was in deplorable condition.

It was located in a part of town that I would euphemistically call "challenging". It looked like the set of a post-apocalyptic movie – nothing but rubble, sand, gravel and concrete buildings in various stages of decay. My new building was in rough shape. The units needed new paint, floors and appliances before they were ready to rent. Half of them didn't even have doors. The swimming pool and tennis courts had deteriorated into unrecognizable bogs, in need of complete restorations. As if that wasn't quite enough to worry about, the parking lot needed to be re-paved, the office needed to be remodeled, and security fencing needed to be installed.

It might sound like such a run-down building would be totally uninhabitable, but there were a few scattered residents in some of the units. Most of them were homeless squatters; the few who made rent payments earned that money through the sale of illicit substances.

Something had to be done.

I wanted to clear out the drug dealers as quickly as possible; one by one, I confronted my tenants the moment I spotted suspicious activity. It was during one such confrontation that I got the funniest drug dealer story of my career.

The maintenance man and I were standing outside the door of a suspected drug dealer's apartment. The tenant couldn't have made his place look more like a drug den if he tried – there were mountains of assorted garbage in front of the doors, sheets of tin foil plastered over the windows, and strange, unreadable markings carved into the door. The tenant noticed our knocking, and when the door swung open, I had to take a few steps back; judging from the smell, something had clearly died in there. I launched into my usual drug dealer routine – I told him that drug activity was unacceptable, he told me I was certifiably insane, and no one moved an inch. No one, he insisted, had ever used or sold drugs on the premises, and he was offended that I would even suspect him of such a thing.

Then a car pulled up in front of the unit.

A lone male stumbled out and lumbered over to the tenant's open door. He completely ignored me standing there, as if I were nothing more than a tacky ornamental lawn flamingo, and told the tenant that he was there to buy some cocaine.

No one said anything. The tenant looked from me to the maintenance man and back, as his face slowly turned beet red. Then, without a word, he went back into his apartment and slammed the door. The maintenance man and I burst out laughing; it was all I could do to keep tears from rolling down my face.

Needless to say – thanks to his impatient customer – we were able to get that tenant out quickly. To this day, it's the only time in my career that I've ever had an eviction argument interrupted by a drug deal, but I'm almost glad it happened. In the end, we were actually able to move some relatively normal tenants into that unit.

Drugs aren't normally a laughing matter, and you need to keep your wits about you when you're dealing with any kind of drug activity on a property. If you're going to get through a career in property management, you've also got to learn to keep your sense of humor about you, and find things to laugh about. It's the best way to keep yourself in a good mood and retain your sanity.

CHAPTER THREE

My Date with Phoenix SWAT

I've had a lot of things happen to me over the course of my career, both good and bad, but the best thing that ever happened to me was the time I had an accidental run-in with the Phoenix SWAT team.

Now, to most people, an encounter with a SWAT team sounds like the kind of life-ruining experience that gets a person on a first-name basis with a parole officer. But to me, seeing the SWAT team was like watching a TV show come to life for my own personal amusement. Most of the day-to-day problems I deal with as a property manager – from marijuana dealers to illegal endangered squirrel breeders – can be handled by run-of-the-mill police officers. It takes a special kind of crime to grab the attention of the SWAT team.

As it just so happened, on the day I met the SWAT team, I was acting as a real estate broker in the sale of an apartment building in a challenging part of town. It was the sort of place that you would bring your gun, but not your children. I did have a gun on me, in fact; whenever I head into an especially challenging area, I bring my trusty Colt 380 along. Despite having the same name as an adorable male baby horse, it's a deadly weapon. I've never actually had to pull it out, but when things get tense, it makes me feel better to know that I can slowly reach towards my pocket and pretend I'm in an Old West standoff. Not every state allows for the carrying of concealed weapons, so be sure to check your local laws before you pack your pistol in the morning.

The unit I was dealing with at the time was a small one – just six units – with an industrial-sized attached garage. As it turned out, that garage was the source of the trouble. One of the tenants had gotten permission to use it for his car detailing business, but at some point he'd made a minor adjustment to his business plan and started using the garage as an illegal drug distribution center. The owner/manager was probably aware of the situation, but he liked collecting the rent money too much to say anything. He thought that if he just tried his hardest to ignore the situation, it would all resolve itself and no one would ever come to any harm.

He couldn't have been further from the truth.

The investor I was talking to was looking for a small apartment, and he thought the large garage would be perfect for storing excess inventory for his business. I thought it best not to mention the drug business that was currently occupying the space; they would be evicted before the buyer ever took possession. In any case, the drug dealers seemed like nice people, as far as remorseless narcotics pushers went.

The building itself was no palace; the only parts of it that didn't need repair were the parts that had fallen down entirely. What made the place such an attractive purchase was the fact that its remarkably low price would leave the buyer with plenty of money left for repair work. Even still, the two buyers wanted to see what they were getting themselves into. With the building's owner in tow to answer any questions, the four of us set off for a tour of the property.

Our first stop was the garage. It contained all the usual sorts of garage-related things – concrete floors, cars, scattered tools and crude shelves. It also contained a not-so-usual array of twelve people hanging around, who seemed to lack any legitimate form of gainful employment. I'd like to think that they were there to be friendly, but in reality, they were there to keep an eye on us. Luckily, the buyers didn't seem to notice that anything was amiss, and the tour continued without incident.

We proceeded to the units, some occupied, and some empty. Whenever we did come across a resident, it was not a pretty pic-ture. It was tough to tell which was at a further stage of decay – the units, or the tenants themselves. Mummified renters aside, the tour went well, and when we'd finished with the last unit we decided to go outside and take a look at the front and side of the building.

That's when the fun began.

The day had blossomed into cool, sunny spring weather by the time we went outside, and – miracle of miracles – the buyers still seemed interested in the building. Life was good for everyone. We looked over the front of the place, and then turned to walk around to the side.

That was when I found myself staring down the barrel of an M-16 rifle.

Now, not everyone gets to play with a toy like an M-16, and the man on the other end of the gun was certainly not just anyone. He was dressed in black from head to toe, with a hood over his face and the letters "SWAT" printed across his back. An assertive voice told me to get on the ground, and I did as I was told.

The place was swarming with SWAT. They were pouring out of cars, vans and helicopters, descending on the building like ants at a picnic. I'd seen SWAT raids in movies, but I always figured I was more likely to win the lottery or get eaten by a man-sized shark than I was to witness a raid first-hand. I turned my head to take in the action; I didn't want to miss a second of it.

Bang! A stun grenade went off in the garage. By this point, I was quite confident that the Phoenix SWAT was not here to look into buying the property.

A few minutes later, we were allowed to stand back up. The neighbourly folks from the garage had been handcuffed and placed in a single-file line, some of them still bleeding from the stun grenade. My companions were visibly shaken, but I was trying to fight back a grin – to the police, I must have looked like a small child unwrapping an excessively expensive gift on Christmas morning. I wanted to know everything. What's going on? Who are you? Can I please, please hold your gun? Is it too late to make a major career change?

The policeman and his very large gun told me to be quiet, but he assured me that someone would come along to answer my barrage of questions shortly.

While we waited, I gently informed the building owner that there might have been some illegal activity taking place in his building. He was not amused.

Eventually, someone from the SWAT team marched over and demanded to see ID. Once we'd assured him that we were not the city's dorkiest drug dealers, I joked that we'd just happened to be in the wrong place at the wrong time. He, too, was not amused.

The officer quickly tired of me, and we were left alone in our designated spot once more. I was still trying to hold in my excitement. Seeing a SWAT raid in person had been a prominent item on my bucket list; now, I was just one trip to the moon away from completing it. I can see how my enthusiasm might be mistaken for complete and utter drooling-into-my-padded-walls lunacy, but anyone who had been there would understand. These men had better training, sharper efficiency and much bigger guns than anyone I'd seen in action so far. It was enthralling.

Finally, the drug raid came to a close. The dealers were bound and cuffed, sitting on the sidewalk, waiting to be loaded into vans like drugged cattle. The SWAT were standing about, dealing with whatever sorts of thing need to be dealt with after raiding a drug-distributing garage. My now ex-buyers took off; the moment police said they could leave, they dashed to their cars and drove off as fast as they possibly could in the presence of a major branch of law enforcement. I stayed behind for a moment with my seller, and gently broke the news to him that we might have lost the sale.

He was not amused.

I walked back to my car still riddled with excitement. I quit my job that very night, and by the next week, I was enrolled in police training for a new career on the SWAT team.

I wish.

I stayed in real estate, and the memory stayed with me forever. I concluded my perfect date with the SWAT team that evening with dinner at my favorite restaurant, certain my encounter with the team was destined to be little more than a one-day fling.

If you were paying attention to the chapter titles, you know that isn't true. More to come!

CHAPTER FOUR

"Where's the Rent?" And "No Speak English"

You never really know who you're renting to. Sure, you can meet the prospective tenants and run background checks on the name that goes down on the lease, but no matter how careful you are, you can never be quite sure who you're going to find on the other side of a unit's front door.

For instance, let's imagine that you've rented a unit to a young lady. She's polite, responsible and definitely feminine, and only her name goes down on the lease. You might be surprised, then, to inspect her apartment six months later and discover burly young man in there, living by himself. Unless you've got a shapeshifter on your hands, you've just witnessed the tail end of a real estate love story gone awry – at some point, the young lady you rented to moved her soul mate into the apartment with her. Later on, when she'd realized that she didn't want to share her home with this smelly, burping creature, she'd made a break for it – probably shimmying down a crude bedsheet ladder in the dead of night – leaving her heartbroken lover to live in the apartment by himself.

Finding one star-crossed twenty-something replaced with another isn't even close to the worst thing you'll find. Sometimes – and I will never, for the life of me, understand how this happens – you'll rent out an apartment to another upstanding young single, not suspecting a thing. You never see a significant other coming or going from their apartment, so you feel pretty confident that you know who you have living in the unit. Then, one day, you open the door and discover that the place is filled with random strangers you've never seen before. Did your tenant found a cult in their living room? Did they surrender their home to their knitting club? Has your original resident been dividing by mitosis to create a room full of people? You might never know.

But, as horrible and awkward as those scenarios are, there's another occurrence that tops them. This vanishing act usually begins with a couple; they're clean-cut and professional, with gleaming credit scores and rental histories. Maybe they're even looking to start a family. You have no qualms about signing these people up for an apartment. Then, the first time you inspect their place, you realize they may have been a bit overzealous about starting that family, because they have three dozen illegal immigrants camping out in their apartment. You've been duped. That nice couple you thought you were renting to was just a front for an immigration scam, and now you've got an illegal drop house on your property. Great.

Then, as always, there are the drug dealers. It's a similar story – you meet and sign on some prospective tenants who aren't obviously shifty-eyed criminals, and then you later inspect the apartment to find a full-scale Breaking Bad imitation inside. Once again, you've been had. Your responsible, model tenants were just a front for an industrial meth factory.

So what are you supposed to do now? There's no need to panic. Most of the time, you won't even notice that your original tenants have performed a vanishing act and brought in new tenants to take their place – the rent keeps getting paid, the neighbors don't complain, and there are no obvious foul odours emanating from the place. When you do happen to notice that this is going on, make a point of calling the new tenants into your office. They never actually show up, of course, so be sure to drop by the apartment with the paperwork and keys that they'll need to become a legitimate tenant. Everyone stays happy.

Sometimes, though, things don't go quite that smoothly. Sometimes, the mystery residents who show up in other peoples' units don't see a reason why they should pay any rent. And since these charming freeloaders aren't paying for the place, they also don't have any qualms about letting four or five dozen of their closest friends turn the interior into a makeshift nightclub. These sorts of apartments aren't difficult to spot; all you need to do is follow the trail of neighbor complaints, empty beer cans, pizza boxes, miscellaneous garbage and broken glass. By the time you get into the apartment, it may or may not have any window panes left, which also helps with identification.

The first time you drop in on your new two-bedroom permanent party, you should ask to speak to the original tenants. The new tenants will invariable introduce themselves as the siblings, parents, cousins, friends, coworkers or casual acquaintances of the original tenants, and promise to leave them your message. You will never hear a reply. The second time you stop by the apartment, the intruders will inform you that they live in the apartment now, despite the fact that their names don't appear on the lease and their money doesn't appear in your pocket each month. Use any measures necessary to get those kinds of people out.

Sometimes, the tenant deception is more subtle. I'll meet with a lovely couple and their only child, and sign them to a lease. Then, out of nowhere, four or five more children appear. I wasn't born yesterday, and neither were they – my tenants had apparently forgotten all about them when they filled in the lease paperwork. It's not always confined to children, either; sometimes, the new couple invites the entire extended family to move in with them. That might not seem like much of a problem if they're a quiet family, but in the state of Arizona, where building owners pay for water, sewage and trash, more people means less money. A couple that secretly moves their two children in will double the cost, and a couple that moves in everyone they share even a shred of DNA with can wipe out your profits. Fortunately, this sort of situation isn't tough to spot – no matter how well-behaved someone's children are, the neighbors are going to notice if you've got ten of them.

Not every problem is as innocent as a handful of extra children – as I mentioned before, sometimes you come across drop houses filled with twenty or thirty illegal immigrants. Ironically, these fugitives from the law are some of the neatest and quietest tenants you could ask for – the only way you'll find out the drop house exists is if someone slips up and a neighbor gets suspicious. Criminal activity aside, the worst thing about these houses is the toll they take on the apartment – thirty grown adults living in a two-bedroom apartment isn't easy on the doors, appliances, floors or hinges. As a rule, I try not to be a miserable, heartless human being, but those kind of tenants have to go.

Then, of course, there are the drug dealers. I've talked about them at length in chapter two, but I'll mention it again here: you do not want drug dealers as tenants. The worst situation I ever dealt with was a meth lab apartment that didn't want to stop being a meth lab apartment. In retaliation, the tenants set the building on fire, and the tenants next door narrowly avoided being barbecued. The owner of the building fixed the damage with the insurance payout, but it's not an experience I would ever care to repeat.

You're probably wondering how, exactly, to go about confronting these violators of sacred lease agreements. Squirt guns? First extinguishers? Overturned chairs and a whip? It's usually a little simpler than that. Ninety-nine times out of a hundred, if you confront an illegal tenant about their presence in courts, prison, or deportation they just disappear and it is easier for everyong. It's like shining light on a cockroach – they scatter.

On the odd occasion that your tenant doesn't head for the hills, you may need to get creative. Making the person's activities public knowledge is a good place to start; a drug dealer's customers may get skittish if the landlord is breathing down their necks. Calling the police on these stubborn troublemakers doesn't necessarily work; making an arrest means going to the effort of setting up a surveillance operation, and the police aren't usually willing to do that unless you've got a major drug production underway. I've even hired security guards to sit on a chair outside a drug dealer's apartment in shifts for twenty-four-hours a day. None of the dealer's customers are too eager to purchase drugs in front of a uniformed security officer, and the dealer usually leaves as soon as his customers stop coming.

There have been a few industrious and misguided drug dealers who actually offered to pay their rent in illegal wares. I have never accepted. Apartments in those challenging areas also attract the sorts of women who conduct business mainly at night, and those women have also offered to pay their rent with a variety of interesting services. Intriguing? Of course. Have I ever taken one of those ladies up on it? Of course not. I've dealt with a lot of these women over the years, and come up with a general rule about them: strippers make good tenants. They sleep all day, stay out at night, and make sure the rent gets paid. Hookers make bad tenants. They bring a string of seedy clients and bad boyfriends traipsing through your building, and most of them aren't considerate enough to keep up with their rent payments.

As I mentioned, the wares of hookers didn't interest me, but I have, however, accepted one non-monetary rent payment in my career – a 1965 hard-top cherry red Mustang. It originally belonged to a nice little family that lived in one of my units. One day, the father pulled me aside and told me that he was going to jail for six months; it could have been for anything from petty theft to public masturbation – I didn't ask. The man did not want to return from jail to find his family living on the streets, and he asked me if I would accept the car as payment for six months of rent. The car was in great shape, and after a little fixing up, I presented it to my daughter as a gift.

Then she had me sell it and buy her something trendier. Kids.

After all these stories of extra tenants, I have one story about an apartment that had too few tenants. I went into an apartment in one of my fancier buildings, right in the middle of a very nice area of town, and found absolutely no one home. The furniture was neat. The aquarium fish were healthy. There was even food in the fridge. The only thing missing, in fact, were the people. My manager and I kept an eye on the place – it was filled with dishes, clothes, toys and all the other odds and ends that human beings generally relied on to survive their daily lives – but nothing was ever touched. In Arizona, when you suspect that a tenant has made himself permanently scarce, you must stick up a 10-day abandonment notice on his door to see if anyone responds to it. The ten days came and went. When the ten days are up the landlord is required to keep the contents of the apartment in storage, just in case the tenant went on a spontaneous lengthy vacation. The contents of most abandoned apartments aren't worth the price of renting the storage locker, but this house had such high-quality contents that I left them in the apartment for another thirty days. Still, no one showed up to claim anything.

When the contents of the apartment legally became mine, I'll admit, I actually claimed a beautiful oak desk for myself. My staff got second pick of the items, and the little that remained went to charity. To this day, I don't know what happened to those tenants. They might have all come down with total amnesia on the same day, or they might have been superheroes using the place as a cover until evil reared its ugly head again. Whatever the case, I very much enjoyed the desk.

The funniest tenants you'll get, though, don't lie about their numbers or whereabouts – in fact, they're painfully honest. If you're feeling overwhelmed on the job, and you need a good laugh, go track down a tenant who's missed a rent payment – ask him why he hasn't paid you. Whatever comes out of his mouth is almost guaranteed to give you a hearty chuckle. Now, I'm not a heartless man. If someone came to me and explained that they'd had to spend the money on emergency medical bills for their sick child, I would absolutely work out a deal with them right away. But when a dazed-looking young man stammers that he spent his rent money on car maintenance, I have a hard time digging up any sympathy. I hope the backseat of that man's car was comfortable, because he was almost certainly reduced to sleeping in it after his eviction.

It's not always cars that eat up precious rent money, either. Sometimes it's vacations. Or friends. Or clothes. Or drugs. Yes, you read that correctly. Sometimes, a very special kind of tenant will come out and tell you that they are unable to afford their place of residence because they spent all their money on illegal drugs. They are always shocked when you proceeded to tell them that you'll have to evict them.

Don't do drugs, kids. Stay in school.

Another failed 'Get out of Rent Free' card that got played in the 1990s was the 'No Speak English' card. In the early 90s, for the first time, Arizona saw an enormous influx of illegal Spanish-speaking immigrants. It was almost a trend – like Pogs or Beanie Babies, but it was a national problem. We got plenty of these Hispanic immigrants in our buildings, and for the most part, they were model tenants. Some of them were less than honest about the number of children they had, but on the whole, they were a quiet and well-behaved group. They were normally too shy to bring anything but a major maintenance issue to my attention, and they weren't nearly as demanding as other tenants.

Back in those days, no one was learning Spanish. In my school days, the schools mistakenly thought that French was a useful language, and they forced it upon us despite the millions of Spanish-speakers living just a few miles to the south. Today – thanks to my Hispanic tenants – I know a few phrases, though twenty years of academic study of the language has failed to make me anything close to fluent. Anyone looking to go into property management would be wise to sign up for a few classes; the phrase 'Donde la renta?' (Where's the rent?) will be particularly handy.

Now, sometimes, a Hispanic tenant would get behind on the rent. It happens to people from every race and background. But when I'd go to the door to collect money, the tenants suddenly didn't know a word of English. How had they managed to fill out all the English-language paperwork to get on the lease? It was a mystery, because the people at the door spoke only a steady stream of rapid-fire Spanish. I didn't have anyone bilingual on my staff at the time, so, naturally, we would just speak English louder, hoping to get our point across. It seemed hopeless – we were yelling in English, they were shouting back in Spanish, and it didn't look like anyone was going to get paid.

Then, all of a sudden, they would slip.

These tenants always did speak English, and if you kept arguing with them long enough, they'd accidentally let it show. They might answer one of your English questions, or they might answer – in English – a question asked by one of their English-speaking family members within the apartment. The game was up, and they were caught – they'd either pay up or leave. Once managers began to get wise to the 'No Speak English' tactic and hired bilingual employees, it became a moot point, and rent needed to be paid. There was no need to evict these families. You'd march down to their door, notice in hand, only to find a spotless empty apartment; they'd packed up and left in the middle of the night, without a fuss.

Ultimately, you're in this business to make money, and that means collecting rent from orderly tenants. Sometimes you'll have too many tenants, and sometimes you won't have any at all. You might find one tenant switched for another, or one couple might swindle you into playing host for three dozen people. Questionable goods and services get offered up instead of money, and rent payments get lost to planes, trains, automobiles and little bags of powder. Rent negotiations turn into bilingual cultural clashes. But through it all, you've just got to keep asking:

"Where's the rent?"

CHAPTER FIVE

Cockroaches and Termites

Bugs are an unfortunate fact of life. They outnumber humans, and so long as we continue to provide them with food, shelter, warmth, water and bug-related superhero franchises, those creepy crawlies are here to stay. And unless you plan on being the property manager of an Arctic research base, you too going to have to deal with bugs.

One of the most common insects any property manager has to deal with is the common cockroach. Those things can survive in outer space, and in the irradiated wreckage of a nuclear blast, but their favourite place to live seems to be in the garbage and filth of someone's unkempt hovel of an apartment. My stories of cockroaches and the people who unknowingly breed them would look more at home in a B-movie horror script than a real estate book.

In fairness, not everyone who finds a stray cockroach lingering under the refrigerator is an unwashed goblin. No matter how well you think you've sealed up all the cracks and crannies of a building, those six-legged little monsters always find a way to get in. Ordinarily, coming across one in a tenant's unit is no cause for alarm; a responsible property manager should first restrain the urge to scream and flee like a little girl. He or she should then calmly pick up the phone and call an exterminator to set out poisoned 'roach hotels' and spray the offending cockroaches into oblivion. Usually, that's all it takes to eradicate your tenants' unwanted roommates.

Some tenants, however, are special.

Over the years, I've come across a certain type of tenant that I like to call a "roach breeder". Locating the elusive roach breeder is a tricky process, and ridding your building of his thousands of insects is even trickier. Usually, it starts with complaints from your ordinary tenants. They'll be trying to go about their daily lives, making their meals, raising their children and chasing their lifelong dreams of professional oboe playing when, all of a sudden, they notice that there are cockroaches swarming into their apartment by the dozen from every unseen nook and a cranny. The tenants, not being used to seeing swarms of large brown insects descending on their living space, will promptly place a hysterical call to the property manager – presumably, you. When you inspect the home and fail to find any rotting food, abandoned beverages or unsupervised garbage, you may be tempted to conclude that the roaches are a mysterious, modern-day Biblical plague. This is an understandable mistake.

What you're really dealing with is a roach breeder.

The common roach breeder, in the natural habitat it had established in one of your units, is an unabashed hoarder of every filthy thing they comes across. To this person, food expiration dates are merely useless decorations printed on the labels, and the floor is a perfectly acceptable alternative to a trash can. To a cockroach, the roach breeder's unchecked mounds of garbage are the equivalent of a family-friendly suburb with good schools; newlywed roach couples flock to the horrifying apartment and begin to multiply 100,000 times quicker than rabbits!

Now, so long as the roach breeder maintains this inhospitable indoor swamp, the cockroaches won't wander from his apartment. They know they've got a good thing going; poking their heads out the door means poison, death, cats, rats, dogs, people, brooms, bug spray, insecticide and an appalling lack of rotting garbage. So long as the roach breeder stays put and maintains his personal landfill, his thousands of roaches will be happy and you won't even know he's there. But sometimes, for some reason or another, roach breeders don't stay put. Sometimes they get behind on rent and decide to quietly make themselves scarce. Other times, they wake up one morning and realize that they're living in a knee-high sea of biohazards and mold. And sometimes they don't give a reason for their departure at all; they slip out in the middle of the night leaving no trace of their existence, like secret agents who desperately need to get out of town. Whatever the reason for their departure, the roaches soon notice that their normally steady supplies of stale pizza crusts, spilled soda and unidentifiable take-out food remains have suddenly run dry.

Perhaps understandably, the cockroaches panic. And when they panic, the first thing they do is scope out their next source of food – in your building's other units.

Unlike garden-variety, Sammy-left-a-piece-of-cheese-out-overnight-and-now-we-have-a-cockroach pests, roach breeder infestations cannot be treated with a phone call to the exterminator and a bottle of Lysol. You're dealing with thousands of members of a species that will literally outlast all other life on Earth, and treating them the usual way is going to make you feel like the Sisyphus of Greek mythology fame, forever pushing his metaphorical boulder up the hill. You're never going to win.

What you need to do is get right to the source.

If you currently house or recently housed the foul-smelling lair of a roach breeder, calling the exterminator to deal with it is a great plan – if you've ever wondered what it sounds like when a man passes out from laughing too hard. No exterminator is going to lift a finger to help you until you've done most of the heavy lifting yourself. Yes, that means you're going to have to clean out the roach den. No, it's not going to be pleasant.

There is no haunted house or horror movie in existence which can fully prepare you for what you'll see in the abandoned home of a roach breeder. The mountains of refuse are horrifying in their own right, but it's the blankets of cockroaches on every available surface – on the floors, tables, walls and ceilings – that make the experience uniquely awful. Keep in mind that you'll be going into a semi-dark apartment to keep the creatures out of hiding, and you'd be forgiven for wanting to leap up and take a shower just from reading about it.

Now, I'm no entomologist. I couldn't tell you the scientific names of those cockroaches any more than I could locate the lost continent of Atlantis. But what I have noticed is that these cockroaches seem to come in three different varieties. The first kind are the gigantic, Halloween-decoration-sized roaches that like to take up residence under kitchen counters, on floors, under tables, and anywhere else that gravity allows them to get to. The second variety are the smaller, more aerodynamic variety that prefer to build their brown, granular nests in the cracks between walls and ceilings. These are the cockroaches that will be dropping down on your head from above when you come through the door, so brace yourself for that.

Then there are the sewer cockroaches. These are the types of cockroaches that make you put down the exterminator's phone number and dial up the nearest priest. As their name suggests, these cockroaches make their homes in the sewer, but when they come across a more desirable source of food, they'll happily come streaming out of toilets, showers and sinks to get at it.

Your natural reaction upon walking into a roach den for the first time will be to run out, screaming and crying as you try to brush off any straggling cockroaches. You'll make a few empty threats to change your profession, and then you'll finally settle down to deal with the problem. So how, exactly, are you supposed to deal with the cockroach apocalypse taking place in your building? It's not pretty, but it's simple – you need to roll up your sleeves and clean.

Round up as many people as you can pay to help you, and get everything out of that apartment.

First, the food sources will need to go – that alone will persuade some of the roaches to relocate. Then, haul everything out of the apartment. Every piece of furniture and every household item could be harboring food or roaches, and it all needs to go. Whether you bury it, burn it or launch it into the dark voids of outer space is up to you, but your roach breeding will cease as soon as the place is empty. From there, you can call that exterminator to come and deal with the straggling roaches trying to settle down in your neighboring units.

The worst roach breeder I ever encountered was in a 32-unit building I owned and managed when the televisions show, The Fresh Prince of Bel-Air, was still going strong. I knew the tenant had abandoned the place, but I still had to serve up that magical 48-hours-notice that lets me barge into an apartment whenever I please. I made the mistake of taking my dainty female manager into the place with me. She screamed like we'd stumbled upon a dead body; in fairness the place look like a scene out of Amityville-style murder mystery. We ended up hiring a group of men with stronger arms and stomachs than we had to deal with the mess. To this day, I don't know what they did with any of the contaminated furniture, and frankly, I don't care. So long as I never see any of it again, I'm happy.

Before you start reading up on cockroaches, thinking you'll get ahead of the game by familiarizing yourself, you should know that cockroaches aren't the only insects you'll be dealing with. Bugs of every persuasion just want a safe pile of stale garbage to raise the kids on, and the common housefly wastes no time in laying hundreds of eggs amidst the cockroaches. Those with any knowledge of the housefly life cycle will realize that hundreds and hundreds of fly eggs quickly become hundreds and hundreds of maggots. During the cleanup of one of my most notable roach breeder dens, I can remember picking up a sealed, crusty styrofoam container of what I assumed to be food. I wasn't wrong. On my way to dispose of the container, the lid popped off, sending dozens of white, squirming maggots all over my clothes. I'll admit that I took off through the unit's front door, shrieking like a mythological banshee. I didn't stop until I'd reached my car; a passersby might have thought I was hallucinating as I stripped off my clothes and rubbed antiseptic all over any exposed part of my body.

I quickly learned after the maggoty styrofoam incident that, whenever possible, it's better to hire others than to get your hands dirty. No matter how repulsive a task is, someone out there is always willing to do it for just the right amount of money. You can pay someone to clean out your cockroaches, massage your feet, wash your car, raise your children, and clean out the abandoned possessions of a seasoned hoarder. And, as I soon discovered, for the right amount of money, you can find someone willing to crawl through cold mud on their belly, looking for animal corpses.

Most houses built in the southwestern United States are built on concrete slabs. But sometime, you come across a building that's been raised off the ground with a crawlspace underneath. These crawlspaces are dark, dirty, full of pipes and accessible only through a small door that even Alice in Wonderland wouldn't touch. Every so often, a foul smell strong enough to make babies cry wafts up out of the crawlspace, and I have to hire someone to go down there and sort it out. I'll be honest – I have no idea what causes those problems in the crawlspace. To be even more honest, I don't want to know. There could be broken sewer pipes, dead animals, or an entire lost civilization of people boiling cabbage down there. Whatever it is, I pay someone to squirm through the door and fix it, and I hope to never hear any details beyond that.

If cockroaches and maggots don't provide quite enough bug-related fun for you, you can always count on termites. If you're dealing with property in a place that builds with wood and doesn't freeze solid every winter, chances are, you're already familiar with termites. Different species of termites prefer different geographical regions, and in the Arizona area, we play host to the subterranean variety of termite that crawls forth from the ground like a zombie. These little beasts make their way up through cracks in the building's concrete slab and climb up the walls to feast on the tasty wooden joints that prevent the roof from falling in, before returning to the underground each night.

Luckily, subterranean termites are easy to detect if you know what to look for. As they chew away at the home you've financially and emotionally invested in, they create little grainy termite tunnels on the surface of the wall. The tunnels look like varicose veins made out of sand, and the longer they are, the worse your termite infestation is. Usually, by the time termite tunnels are spotted, they're only a few inches long.

Like cockroaches and crawlspaces, termite colonies are yet another thing that a property manager can hire someone else to deal with. The exterminator comes out and drills a hole in the concrete slab, and termite poison goes in. The poison clogs up any crack, hole or gap in the concrete that the termites might have been squeezing through, turning their daily commute into a suicide mission. There's no treating part of a slab to solve the problem; termites may have a brain the size of a grain of sand, but even they can figure out how to go around a segment of poisoned concrete. The whole slab has to be treated, and the bigger the building, the more you'll be forking over to the exterminator to put an end to the termite buffet.

The thing about termite infestations is that they're a matter of "when", not "if". Unless you deal with nothing but concrete fallout shelters, the termites are coming to nibble on your property. There's a little game that buyers and sellers play with their termite populations; when you're selling a property, you don't want the termites to be found – for obvious reasons. But when you're buying, you're hoping that the little monsters will show themselves – an unsold property with known termites means the owner has to pay for treatment and provide the seller with a warranty.

I came across the worst termite infestation I ever laid eyes on just a few months ago, when I was out inspecting a pair of four-plexes that was for sale by a non-profit. The non-profit had purchased the buildings five years prior, when the government – as governments often do during devastating economic downturns – ran out of money and put an end to their funding. With no other obvious options, the non-profit had boarded up the building as best they could, and they remained like that for five years until one of my clients offered to buy them. Before any deal could be signed, however, my client sent me out to inspect the place.

The images that come to mind when you think "abandoned building" are exactly what I found myself looking at. The property had overgrown grass, broken and boarded windows, damp floors and plenty of dust – it was exactly what you might expect in a place no one has set foot in in half a decade. What you might not be expecting to find in an abandoned place in an upscale area of Scottsdale is the worst termite infestation of my entire career. Forget six-inch-long termite tubes; these ones easily stretched more than eight feet, winding their way up the walls and dangling down from the ceiling like jungle vines. At best guess, there were fifty or more individual termite tubes in one room alone. A person unfamiliar with termites might have been forgiven for thinking an enormous sandy tree had grown through the walls. We called in a man who dealt with termites for a living, and even he was at a loss for words as he surveyed our termite jungle.

No matter how careful or you, or how many exterminators you hire, remember that bugs are always going to be a part of the real estate business. They may not sign leases or pay rent – in fact, they'll cost you money – but they'll move in and out of your buildings more often than people do. You can scream, you can flee and you can cry, but in the end, the only way to get rid of them is to deal with them.

So listen closely for the patter of six little feet. And always keep an eye out for roach breeders.

CHAPTER SIX
No One Lives There

How do you know when a unit is occupied?

To most people, the answer is usually somewhere along the line of "someone is living there". There is food in the fridge, clothes in the closet, light in the windows, and someone comes to the door when you ring the bell. People in the real estate business, however, have a completely different definition of "occupied" that goes a little something like this: a unit is occupied if someone is paying rent for it. That's all there is to it. I frankly don't care if you've rented the unit as a spare office, or as extra storage space for your plastic lawn ornament collection. So long as you're quiet, law-abiding, and handing me a check every month the place is yours.

This seems like a simple policy, but a staggering number of my tenants seem to disagree, because every so often I get a phone call that goes a little like this:

Woefully Stupid Tenant: "Hi, it's John Doe calling from apartment number five in that building you manage, and my shower is broken. I need someone to come and fix it."

Me: "That's not possible. No one lives in that apartment."

Apparent Ghost Living in Unit Five: "What do you mean? I live in that apartment! I'm one of your tenants."

Me: "You can't possibly be living in that apartment. I haven't received any rent payments for that apartment in two months, and if someone was living there, they would be paying rent."

At that point, the line usually goes quiet while I calmly explain that plumbers – for whatever reason – insist on being paid with real, actual money, and without monthly rent payments, I don't have any real, actual money to give them for repairs. After that, some ghost-tenants get very sheepish, very quickly, and catch up on their rent the minute the line goes dead. Others seem to believe that arguing with me and threatening will somehow negate their unpaid rent and get their shower fixed. That tactic never works out.

Now, by law, I am required to do those repairs. I can't force a tenant to resort to sponge baths, no matter how far they've fallen behind on their rent. But the law says absolutely nothing about having sarcastic phone conversations with tenants, and I like to exercise that right whenever the opportunity presents itself.

Sassy phone conversations with tenants aren't my only problem with Alexander Graham Bell's famous invention. You see, back in the early 90's, when people still wore acid-washed jeans in public and dinosaurs roamed the earth, cellphones hadn't yet taken off in popularity. What was a young drug dealer to do, if he didn't want to be traced through his personal landline?
Why, he used a payphone, of course.

In those days – and especially in those interesting areas I chose to work in – not everyone could afford a landline. Instead, a public payphone would be set up on the building's premises by telephone moguls who made their fortunes twenty-five cents at a time. These phones were placed on the properties on a lease basis, and there was no breaking a lease when a building changed hands; when you bought a building, you bought its laundry and phone leases along with it.

Having access to a telephone isn't a bad thing, but when drug dealers are lined up by the receiver to arrange deals at all hour of the day and night, the phone has to go. I knew that if I cut off the dealers' only convenient means of communicating with customers, most of them would be inclined to pack up and find somewhere more accommodating to live while they waited for the invention of the smart phone. As it turned out, calling the phone company didn't help; they didn't particularly care if their phone aided in the daily sale of three tons of heroin, so long as they had a box of shiny coins to collect at the end of each day. If I wanted the problem solved, I would need to take matters into my own hands.

If you've been paying attention to the previous five chapters, you've probably realized by now that property managers sometimes need to get creative. You might also have suspected that good managers sometimes need to bend, break, and enthusiastically trample on the rules to get things done. My solution to the drug dealer phone problem was definitely a trampling.

It was so simple that it was almost brilliant. Every night, I'd slip out of my office to the payphone, cut through the cable, and walk off with the receiver. In the morning, the drug dealers would find themselves cut off from their eager customers, and would contact the phone company for repairs. When the new receiver was hooked up again, I'd slip out in the dead of night and cut it off again.

Drug dealers may be at least seven kinds of stupid, but they're not the kind of stupid that fails to get suspicious when the phone is vandalized seven days in a row. They'd come by my office, accusing me of the dastardly deed, but I'd always deny it until they got bored of arguing and found something better to do. Like fossil fuels and sign-language-trained gorillas, there is a finite supply of telephone receivers in this world; eventually, the phone company realized that they were losing money on all the phone repairs, and they'd voluntarily remove the phone. As I predicted, the loss of the phone usually meant a mass fleeing of the building by those skinny, twitchy individuals with unusually secretive jobs.

Now, I'm not about to advocate law-breaking. I spent most of my career focused on evicting criminals, and I don't want to spend the money I earned all those years on a series of various lawsuits. But I am going to admit to one other act of vandalism I carried out in the interest of rent payments. When I had tenants in Arizona who came to believe that they didn't owe rent money in exchange for their homes, I'd sneak up to the roof in the middle of summer and disconnect the air conditioning. This isn't just any ordinary summer, either, where a pair of shorts and a well-placed desk fan are all the relief you need. In the middle of a Phoenix summer, you can carry out all of your stovetop cooking on the sidewalk, and people start to seriously wonder if they can go out in public wrapped in ice packs. They took air conditioning very seriously there, and by law, the A/C had to be fixed within 24 hours of the first complaint – unless, of course, I needed to order in a new part. The tenants rarely had any serious reaction to the air conditioning fiasco – most of them had nowhere else to go, and they hardly thought to blame me for the problem – but getting petty revenge on my rent-dodging tenants eased my frustrations.

I have one thing to say before I move on: please, don't ever, ever do that. As a legion of older relatives have no doubt told you, "do as I say, not as I do". I do not have words to describe how illegal this is, and you will absolutely face steep consequences if you're caught. Sabotaging air conditioning units is wrong. Finding creative ways to drive out unwanted tenants is not. Use your imagination.

The limits on how you can treat tenants also very by state. In Arizona, it's possible to have a police constable come and escort your disgraced tenant from the premises while a maintenance man changes the locks. The tenant is only allowed to take what they can carry – to get the rest of their things back, they are required to call and set up a time to collect their things, under heavy supervision. If they never call to make that appointment, their possessions become my possessions – I can keep them, auction them, or throw them into the sea as an offering to Poseidon if I want to. Evictions in Arizona follow a certain routine, and it usually works out just fine.

At least, all of my evictions worked out fine, until I met this one family. They weren't dangerous, but they were rough around the edges, and I had plenty of reason for wanting them out of my building. They made such trouble for me that a constable-escorted eviction seemed to be my only real option, and when the day came everything appeared to go off without a hitch. They left the premises, and the lock on their first floor apartment was changed. All I had left to do was wait for them to call me about collecting their things.

Instead of calling, however, this family chose to take a much more direct approach. Rather than wait for an official, supervised meeting, they simply ran around the back of the building, pried open the window, and climbed back into their living room.

My tolerance for trespassing is even thinner than my tolerance for unpaid rent, and I had the police on the phone in moments. But by the time the boys in blue showed up, the unwanted family had slipped back out the window and into the night.

This quickly turned into a cycle. Three or four times a day, the family would scurry back in through the broken window and resume living in their old apartment, as if they weren't breaking the law by being there. I would phone the police, and they'd come running, but the family would be gone by the time they arrived. I knew I couldn't continue this pattern forever if I didn't want to turn into the Phoenix's police department's new 'boy who cried wolf'. If I was going to get those tenants out, I had to get creative.

I hate to sing my own praises, but I can be awfully clever when the situation arises. The next time I spotted the family slipping out the back window, I called a maintenance man to take all of the doors and windows off the apartment. When they returned, they were horrified – this was not the sort of neighborhood where unguarded possessions stayed put for more than an hour. I knew I'd won when the head of the family sheepishly trotted over to my office;

he conceded defeat, and told me that he and his family would clear out their things at once. True to his word, the family packed up, and I never saw them again.

My sabotage of the apartment's doors was one of my best creative solutions, and it was one that I was well within my rights to do. The phone and the air conditioning were way out in the darkest parts of a legal grey zone, but I got my karmic repayment for the air conditioning vandalism when I was managing a building in Phoenix, years later.

The building in question was a 150-unit building that ran on a central chiller system. These central chiller systems – which might be unique to Arizona– are water-based systems that provide air conditioning, electricity and hot water to the building. The owner of the building is required to pay for the services, and generally, the costs of running the chiller are tacked on to the cost of rent. A unit that might cost $400 plus utilities per month in another building goes for $500 per month, with no additional utilities cost. Unless you're putting on a three-hour laser light show in your living room every evening, you're not actually saving money – most tenants simply prefer to have all their expenses on just one bill.

Now, chiller units are human inventions. They're not perfect. Sometimes – particularly if the unit uses the same pipes for air conditioning and hot water – the units break down and need repairs. Keep in mind that breakdowns are an all-or-nothing deal – if one tenant loses air conditioning, all tenants lose it. And, because the universe is a cruel place, repairs to chiller units are rarely minor. Usually, they require some large and complicated part to be shipped in from a remote part of the country.

The chiller in my building broke down when I was the building manager. It didn't break down during a nice, temperate spring day or crisp fall evening, either. Of course not. The chiller died a painful, sputtering death right in the middle of a 115-degree heat wave, leaving tenants without air conditioning, power or cold water.

So how did the tenants react? Did they suck it up and deal with the heat? Move to Alaska? Invest in generators? Stay at their mothers' houses? Of course not – the minute the chiller went down, they got out their cellphones to call the local news and explain that I'd personally broken the chiller with black magic. Things erupted into instant pandemonium – the chiller needed a large and costly part that would take two days to arrive, and the media weren't willing to let the story go until things were up and running again. They camped out outside the apartment, interviewing tenants who firmly believed that they would not survive to see the new part installed, and that the management company had broken the chiller for their own sadistic pleasure.

On our part, all my staff and I could do was hand out fans and bottled water. A few of our more delicate residents had to be put into hotel rooms for the night – that's how bad it was. And, of course, in between opening crates of bottled water, I also had to deal with reporters' microphones in my face. That evening, the building and I graced the 5 o' clock news. Then, the ten o' clock news. I was the main villain in town that night; admittedly, though it wasn't how I'd have chosen to make my television debut, it was still cool to see my face on the screen. Family and friends started calling, telling me that I didn't look nearly as fat on camera as they'd expected, and jokingly asking me why I was so heartlessly barbecuing my tenants. I felt like a reality TV star, without the fake tan or poor decisions.

On the second day, the missing part arrived, the unit was fixed, and the reporters scattered like cockroaches to feed on more interesting stories. I wasn't the only one in my family to struggle with media attention. My brother almost had a few moments of unwanted fame when one of the tenants in a building he was managing murdered her daughter and hid the body. This resulted in a month-long media circus of reporters camped on the sidewalk outside the apartment. They weren't there for him – my brother's name never appeared in the headlines or TV reports – but they stalked the entrances of the building, hoping to catch a rare glimpse of the monstrous woman as she left the apartment. Thankfully, the media attention dried up when the trial started, and no one from our family or management company has dealt with that kind of spotlight ever since.

At the end of the day, real estate is a business; we're there to make sure that the units are occupied and that money keeps flowing in. Sometimes, occupancy becomes an issue: people live in apartments that don't generate any rent revenue, people break back into apartments that they've been sternly told to stay out of, and tenants convince themselves that they're going to die on you before you can get their basic utilities up and running. But you can handle it. Be firm. Be clever. Be proactive.

And above all, be creative.

CHAPTER SEVEN
Felonies and Evictions

No one is perfect. Over a career as a property manager, you'll rent to people with speeding tickets, unresolved family problems, dead-end careers, speech impediments, medical problems, and irrational fears of clowns. Everyone has a flaw or two, but most people still turn out to be good tenants. There's usually no need to worry about the embarrassing moments or failures in a prospective renter's past.

Unless, of course, your prospective renter is a convicted felon.

Early on in my career – at the very first property I ever managed – I learned the hard way that criminals need places to live, too. I'd hired a building manager whose background checks apparently consisted of little more than glancing a person up and down for obvious knife wounds, and she ended up renting to a man who was very clearly a murderer. Now, I don't like to jump to conclusions; I know that anyone – of any age, race, gender or appearance – could have some very literal skeletons in their closet. I didn't declare this man a murderer based on his face or his hairstyle.

It was his teardrop prison tattoo.

For those not familiar with American prison culture, tattoos hold great significance. Unlike suburban teenagers, who decorate their bodies with meaningless, pretty pictures, inmates get tattoos to send very specific messages. A tattoo of a clock with no hands represents a life sentence. A tattoo of the number 14 represents a strong interest in all things that are white supremacist. And a little black teardrop under the eye – like the one on the face of my tenant – means that you've done away with another member of our species.

Needless to say, the murderer in my building was not a good tenant. He'd moved in with his wife, child, pit bulls, and white supremacist beliefs. And with an iron-clad lease, there was no getting him out. The pit bulls were the first of our problems; I'd expressly forbidden the breed in my building; a fact that my manager had apparently overlooked. His two dogs didn't do much to make me rethink my pit bull policy as we had constant reports of them trying to jump over their fence and maul the other tenants.

Not all of my problems with Teardrop Tenant can be blamed on his pets, either. As it turned out, having a white supremacist living beneath a black man caused more than a little tension. He made constant threats to murder his neighbor, none of which he made good on. With the safety of my other tenants at stake, though, I knew I had to get him out as quickly as I could.

Unfortunately for me, aside from threatening to murder his fellow renters, the man was a stellar tenant. His rent was paid in full, on time. All I could do was wait for his lease to run out. When that day finally arrived, I quickly let the tenant know that murderous racists were no longer welcome, and I refused to renew the lease. Of course, once he'd been told that killing was not acceptable in my building, he tried to rally me to his cause by threatening to kill me. You probably won't be shocked to learn that he didn't succeed. In the end, he quietly moved out. He even left me a little souvenir – when I went back into his empty apartment, I found a little doll of myself hung by a long noose from the ceiling.

In fact, the murderous tenant from my first building wasn't the only person to threaten my life. What would a property management career be if it didn't come with empty death threats? Over time, they go from genuinely worrying to routine annoyance; by now, I'm more afraid of pipe leaks and mouse infestations than I am of tenant threats. My exchanges with my would-be murderers have become almost comical.

"You need to fix that window and pay the rent." I said to a tenant who had recently jettisoned one of his possessions out of his apartment through the glass pane.

"No, I'm not going to do that," says the tenant, before providing what he feels is a reasonable alternative, "I'm just going to kill you."

"Okay, gotcha, but you still have to fix the window." It just doesn't bother me anymore.

It's surprising how many of my tenants view murdering their landlord as a "get out of rent free" card. They seem to believe that the best way to cover up their mistakes is to make an even bigger mistake. It's like trying to cover up a dent in your bumper by setting your car on fire. I get tired of it. I own a gun, and I know how to use it; we'll see who wins. Death threats are no obstacle to collecting rent payments, and after a career filled with them, I'm still here.

Not all of my felon tenants have made attempts on my life. Sometimes, the only thing they're a danger to is my career.

I once came upon a building that housed nothing but single males. This was an unusual arrangement, to say the least – it's not often that a building is deemed livable by only one gender. Intrigued, I started to dig into the backgrounds of these men.

That was when I realized the owner was renting exclusively to sex offenders.

Every sexual depravity and crime was represented; the building's residents included everything from Peeping Toms to pedophiles and serial rapists. The owner had been managing the building before I came along, and he apparently had a policy of renting only to those people who graced the national sex offender registry. It wasn't the kind of place where you'd want to raise the kids.

The entire building was a massive, festering pile of liability – I couldn't subject my management company to that. Had one of the sex offenders decided to relapse into his old ways in his apartment, the liability would come down on my head and the building's owner's head. I was one illicit fondle away from having to resign from property management.

Thankfully, the owner had had the good sense to keep his tenants on temporary, 30-day leases. The rule with those leases is that you can give out a 30-day notice that the lease won't be renewed, and the tenant has to pack up and go when the month is up. Every single one of those sex offenders left without a fuss; I assume they found various cracks and crannies to occupy. Today, the building is home to a variety of families, couples, and other "normal" residents.

A bad criminal record isn't the only thing that will keep a tenant out of my apartment buildings. As anyone who has ever been involved in property rental knows, the first thing a responsible manager does is run a credit check on a prospective tenant. Most of the time, everything comes back fine, but sometimes, you get to feel like an archaeologist uncovering a lost city of unpaid bills and apartment evictions. That's the fun part; you get to go back to the tenant and ask them, "Well, why should we rent to you if you didn't pay your rent at the last place?" Try it sometime. The answers are priceless.

When you've got a prospective tenant with a renting history, it's a good idea to call up the previous manager and ask them if you're about to make a horrible mistake by renting to that individual. In the states of Arizona and California, there's a little law about which questions the previous manager has to answer. Legally, you get two questions – "Did this person live here?" and "Would you rent to them again?" You can ask any questions you like – "Does this person routinely host orgies in their bathroom?" "Is this person a shameless psychopath?" "Did this person smuggle livestock into the building in the dead of night?" – but, the only answers you're guaranteed to get are to the two mentioned above: "Yes, the person lived here. Yes, I would rent to them again."

If the other apartment manager tells you "No, I'd never rent to this person again", stop what you're doing and reject their application immediately. Learn from the other manager's mistakes; there's no need for one idiot to make two managers miserable. That said, hearing "yes" on the other end of the line shouldn't make you trip over yourself to approve the application, either. Managers are people, and people lie. The person on the application may be the most horrendous, garbage-hoarding, drug-dealing, rent-avoiding human being you'll ever lay eyes on, and his manager is so desperate to see him gone that he gives you a fraudulent glowing review. Be inquisitive. By law, you're only entitled to ask those two questions, but most managers are willing to talk. They'll tell you all about the times he's helped his elderly neighbour up the stairs, or all the times he's kidnapped the neighbour's baby. They'll give you some indication of what makes the person a good or bad tenant. A cagey manager is a manager with something to hide – that "something" might just be a small fortune in missed rent payments and property damage. You might have to dig around and do your own investigation before you rent to them.

Managers aren't the only ones who lie. Tenants are filled with plenty of their own dishonesty. They all claim to have good credit histories; when you uncover their nearly mathematically impossible credit score, they'll play dumb, as if their dozens of missed rent, car loan, and utility payments somehow slipped their mind. I'm not a heartless man – if you fell behind on bills while trying to keep up with medical bills for your chemotherapy treatments, we can work something out. Most of the time, there's no excuse. The person with the heinous credit history just leaves without argument. And credit checks aren't the only kind of check I run – managers do a job verification check, to ensure that the prospective tenant is employed. Unless you're housing a group of lottery winners, it's tough to pay rent without a job. I've seen unemployed individuals use every trick in the book to skirt this check. Instead of their employer's phone number, they hand you their friend's phone number. They bring you fake pay stubs and fake employment records. Sometimes, the only way to be certain that your tenant actually has a job is to physically drive to their alleged workplace and see if anyone has heard of them.

Tenants also like to lie about their pets. Allowing pets in an apartment is good for business; there are more people who are willing to rent with you if they can bring Fluffy and Fido along. It's the types of beasts that people bring into an apartment that cause problems. For some reason, in a world where literally hundreds of varieties of family-friendly dog breeds are available, people seem to insist on owning the most vicious, attack-prone dogs alive. I do understand that, with proper care and training, these dogs can be gentle giants. However, insurance companies don't agree. Having some sort of pit bull in an apartment will result in your insurance company cancelling the insurance if they find out. But no matter how many times you tell tenants those breeds are banned, you'll still find them by the dozen in your apartment.

Almost all dogs cause problems for a manager. Their barking annoys the neighbors, and their chewing and scratching damages the apartment. If it were up to me, all my tenants would own Chihuahuas – they're barely larger than a rat, and they can bite as hard as their little hearts desire without causing substantial damage to anyone or anything. I don't even bother telling tenants to put their Chihuahuas away during an inspection; it's hard to be afraid of something so small and cute.

Large dogs are another story. Despite insistences that their pet is "just a little sweetie", I require dogs to be shut in a bedroom or a backyard during an inspection. I can't even count how many times a "sweet, harmless" dog has spent the entire duration of the inspection trying to break through the door. Time and time again, I'm reminded of the same joke: A man walks up to a man and a dog and asks "Hey, does your dog bite?" The man says "No", so the guy reaches to pet the dog. He immediately gets bitten, and cries "Hey! I thought you said your dog didn't bite!" The man replies, "Mine doesn't. That's not my dog."

Cats are rarely an issue. I'm allergic to cats, so I don't do the inspections of units that house cats, but they don't cause damage or noise. A hoarder with fifteen or twenty cats crammed in one apartment is alarming for anyone who comes across it, but one or two cats is nothing to worry about.

In fact, most of the pet-related problems in management have nothing to do with the pets themselves. They're problems with the owner. Tenants lie about the breed of their dog, and the quantity of their pets. Tenants who claim they have no interest in pet ownership end up with drooling, half-ton monsters living in their apartments. Those dogs they were "just babysitting" turn into permanent residents. If you're lucky, the smuggled pets will be small and quiet enough that you don't notice the deception.

As any parent will tell you, children are even worse than pets. They're louder. They're messier. They're more destructive. They invite their loud, messy, destructive friends over. Shutting them in kennels or backyards is generally frowned upon. Worst of all, like pets, they're a constant source of deception. Each state has rules for how many children can legally live in a two-bedroom apartment – it's usually around two. Aspiring property managers would do well to learn and enforce their state's rule. Too often, a lease for two children in a two-bedroom apartment turns into ten children sleeping in the bedroom, kitchen, living room, and bathtub. Families make good tenants – they tend to be the most reliable with rent payments and other rules – but too many children in a unit is hard on the place. It's best to catch that early on while you still have un-broken things in the apartment.

Even worse than children, are the drug users. The tweakers. They look like a Praying Mantis having muscle spasms, they keep the sleeping hours of vampires, and they attract a steady stream of undesirable people trickling in and out of the building. You do not want them in your building. Their presence is not a selling point. But as I mentioned in the Drug Dealer chapter, they are notoriously difficult to evict; they deny their drug activity until they're short of breath, and I've seen some of them get angry enough to set the building on fire during their eviction. It's a dangerous, nasty situation, but one way or another, they need to leave.

So I came up with a brilliant idea.

Drug dealers and tweakers may not fear their middle-aged landlords and property managers, but they have very different feelings about the police. But keeping a constant police presence at the apartment is a problem; you can't exactly call them up every time your resident tweaker sticks his nose out the door. What you can do is offer the police a free apartment to use as a precinct office. And that is exactly what I did. The police can come by to get some rest, fill out paperwork in peace and quiet, or just eat and relax. I would keep the place stocked with soda, doughnuts and snacks, and in exchange, I got to see my drug addict and prostitute population collectively soil themselves when they realized there would be police at the building 24/7. The office was the first of its kind in Phoenix, and I made the news for implementing it – the apartment cleaned itself up quickly, and to my knowledge, remains clean and safe to this day.

Drug dealers do their best to be good tenants, so you won't bother them. They always pay their rent, in cash – a trait that I'll admit I love. Once they know you're onto them, some of them offer to pay double the rent if you'll leave them alone. I never take their offers, but I know plenty of other managers must be; nine times out of ten, after I evict them, they pop up in a nearby building and resume their usual dealing. In the old days – I'll confess that I don't know if this still done – the presence of a drug dealer in a building is announced by a simple pair of sneakers. A dealer will knot the laces of a pair of sneakers and throw them up on a telephone line outside the building to proclaim that drugs are being sold in that building. If you're ever walking through the sort of neighbourhood that makes you fear for the safety of your wallet and kidneys, look up – you're bound to see shoes swinging in the breeze from the telephone lines.

It was one such shoe-marked building that gave me the scare of my life. I was presenting a buyer to purchase and manage a building, which meant I had to be along for the inspection. It was only an eight-unit place, but by my estimation, there were at least three units that showed definite signs of drug activity. In fact, the whole neighborhood was probably brimming with narcotics. Every moment we were on the property, those fine, upstanding drug users in the units were outside, carefully watching our every move. Drug addicts started streaming out of nearby buildings to stand outside and watch us. They were like meerkats, standing around wide-eyed and staring. Although my associate and I were armed, we knew better than to push our luck. We climbed back in the car and left, later telling the building's owner that even a well-paid lunatic wouldn't buy or manage the place. I've crossed the place off my radar entirely – I refuse to even so much as drive through the adjacent streets.

I don't like to push my luck. I'm terribly fond of life, and I'm not eager to see it come to an end at the hands of a coked-out mess. If I go to inspect a complex and meth addicts start pouring out of every nook and cranny like ants from a flooded anthill, I calmly explain that I must be at the wrong address, and then I leave and never return. That's no hyperbole, ever; it's really happened. I've been to buildings filled with such upstanding, delightful members of the community that even the police refused to go in.

At the end of the day, property management is a business. I didn't go into it because I take personal delight in the daily goings-on of an illegal narcotics distributer. If a building has solid bones and the potential to be a good investment, you do whatever it takes. You kick out the termites, drug dealers, prostitutes, mice, more drug dealers, rapists, child molesters, murderers and hookers. You put in new floors, doors, windows, paint and appliances. Units that once housed young, twitchy tweakers on a "pay when you feel like it" basis go on to house young families who deposit their rent, and don't require you to get on a first-name basis with the local police. The recovery process isn't always smooth, but it has to be done.

The longer a building stays in poor condition, the tougher it is to rehabilitate it. Bank-repossessed buildings are the worst of the lot. Long after the places empty out, the banks are still preoccupied with counting their money and stomping on their customers' dreams; by the time anyone thinks to nail plywood over the windows, you'll be almost out of windows to protect. Under bank care, I've seen buildings bleed out almost three-quarters of their value. Air conditioning units, copper pipes, wires, siding, and appliances are stripped from the building and hauled down to the local recycling unit to be converted into drug money. Most popular is copper. Despite being so worthless we actually use it to mint pennies, copper is a drug addict's favourite currency. They're willing to burrow into walls like human termites, just to root out a few cents' worth of the stuff. Because copper is frequently employed to make water pipes, and copper thieves are so rarely professional plumbers, water damage is a concern. The thief cuts out sections of the pipe and bolts, leaving the building to soak up the gushing water like a piece of soggy cereal. Nobody benefits from this.

The worst copper pilfering I've ever seen was in a building littered with vacant units. I wandered into one of these apartments to inspect it. Everything looked neat, clean, and in order.

I was all set to leave when I noticed the hole in the kitchen wall.

The hole was four feet by three feet, big enough for a man to crawl through, and stepping through it into the next apartment eventually turned into a chain of seven apartments, all connected by the conspicuous holes in the wall. A copper thief had tunneled his way through seven units, stripping all of them of copper. I was almost too impressed to be angry. The thief had spent a great deal of time and caused thousands upon thousands of dollars' worth of damage to pull this off, and in the end, he was never caught. What kinds of coppery riches did he get away with, you ask?

Probably somewhere between twenty and one hundred dollars.

Copper stands at the top of the petty thief target podium, but A/C units are a strong second. Trying to hold onto A/C units in a rough area is like trying to hang onto a handful of hot sand; they slip through your fingers no matter what you do. Thieves cut locks, jump fences, scale fences, foil security, sneak past cameras, back-flip over barriers, and somersault across roofs to claim their prize. It doesn't matter when you install the units – rooftop units and window units go missing all the same. Some thefts leave me with no choice but to conclude that acrobats and witchcraft were involved. And, like everything else, the problem is worse the longer the place is abandoned – if a bank-repossessed building comes with a single A/C unit intact, count yourself lucky.

Felons, criminals, drug addicts, thieves, sex offenders, and the unemployed all need places to live, and you can be sure that they'll try to move into your buildings. A good manager has to be alert and keep destructive tenants out of the apartments. Keeping your units safe and desirable means you may have to be blunt. You'll have to be assertive. You might need to get creative. Do what you need to do. If there's one tip you should take away from this chapter, it's this:

Always keep an eviction notice handy. You never know who's moving in.

CHAPTER EIGHT
Apartment Managers

In every profession, there are good employees and bad employees. Some nurses can single-handedly save lives; others struggle to put a bandage on correctly. Some lawyers see their clients walk out of slam-dunk murder trials as free men; others watch helplessly as their clients receive twenty-year sentences for littering. Some teachers inspire Nobel Prize winners; others drive their students to drop out of high school. Apartment managers suffer from the same differences in quality. I've met a lot of managers throughout my career – some were excellent, and some were hardly fit to even live in an apartment.

The first manager at the first apartment complex I ever bought was a typical little old lady, right down to her blue-tinted hair. Years of smoking had left her with a voice that sounded as if she was gargling hot tar when she spoke, and she was so small and frail that I worried we may have to nail her shoes to the ground every time a high wind picked up. She did an okay job of managing – she wasn't fantastic, but she wasn't criminally negligent either. Before I'd stepped in to purchase the building, it had been the property of the

Government of the United States, which explained a great deal of her laziness.

I should explain. If you didn't grow up with black-and-white televisions and rotary phones, you may not be old enough to remember the savings and loan crisis of the late 1980's and early 1990's. The crisis had its roots in a series of poor decisions and bad investments made by foolish people around the world; explaining all of it could be a book in and of itself. I'll try to give you an abridged explanation of the crisis: In the 1980's, Ronald Reagan's administration changed a tax law that promptly led the entire real estate market to collapse. Savings and loan associations across the country had been backing real estate loans, so they, too, promptly collapsed. The government then founded the Resolution Trust Company, which divested assets from ruined savings and loan associations, starting with the most expensive properties.

The first properties to be snapped up were the swanky Class A properties, most of which eventually ended up being sold to the governments' wealthiest friends. The Class B properties were the next to go, and by 1993, when I was ready to buy, they finally got around to selling off their affordable Class C properties. I bought a 44-unit building from the RTC, and the blue-haired manager came with the property. Calling her an 'apartment manager' is actually a generous use of the term; in reality, she was more of a glorified babysitter. So long as she kept the building from burning to the ground, she collected her paycheck, and that was not the sort of attitude I was looking for in a manager.

Now, at the time, I knew absolutely nothing about real estate, management or property ownership. I knew wine. The only exposure

I'd had to the world of real estate was my brother, and he and I weren't exactly having heart-to-heart telephone chats every night. So I blundered into the business blindly, scoffed at Grandma Manager, and attempted to apply my hard-won wine-sales knowledge to management: I would befriend the tenants, and they would do what I wanted.

Grandma Manager laughed at me, and told me how naïve I was being. Naturally, I didn't listen. I was convinced that if I treated the tenants as buddies, they would be scrambling over each other to submit their rent payments early each month. I spared no effort in befriending my tenants. At the height of my foolishness, I actually purchased and distributed pressed fire logs to all of the units for Thanksgiving. Things seemed to be paying off – with each passing day, the tenants warmed up to me, and I was convinced that the forty-four of them were going to be my new best pals.

Unfortunately, I had forgotten one crucial detail. Friends don't jump at the chance to make full rent payments to their friends every month. No, not at all. Friends expect discounts. Friends expect friends to look the other way if they skip out on their rent payments for a few months. Friends expect friends to get maintenance men into their apartment the moment the shower starts to make funny noises. Befriending the people in your building doesn't make them into good tenants; it makes them into entitled, arrogant nightmares who don't think twice about exploiting your kindness.

Eventually, Grandma Manager got tired of laughing at my mistakes and she quit. I needed a new manager, but I knew nothing about hiring a good one. After a lengthy search, I came across a thoroughly psychotic woman, and promptly decided to put her on the payroll.

Hiring Psycho Manager was, as you may have guessed, one of the biggest mistakes of my early career. Right from the beginning, she and I clashed. We argued about everything, names were called, insults were thrown, and competence was questioned. At the heart of the conflict was one simple disagreement: I wanted her to actually work to earn her paycheck, and she wanted to collect it for doing nothing. After a few short months, she still wasn't doing anything productive, and we both knew that I had little choice but to fire her. Instead of storming off the property hurling profanities, however, or leaving the classic bag of flaming dog excrement on my doorstep, Psycho Manager decided to get creative with her send-off.

Around the time I fired her, we had a lot of empty units that we were in the process of filling. Screening applicants for apartments was the manager's job, and she decided to put together a living collage of the worst examples of humanity for me to enjoy after she'd gone. She rented exclusively to terrible human beings. Bad credit history? You're in. Huge, vicious pack of dogs? Of course. Families with more children than I thought one woman was capable of producing? Obviously. Murderers? Right this way, sir. By the time she was finished, the apartment was fit to be the subject of a bad Lifetime documentary, and I had no way of getting any of these people out until their leases were up or they stopped making rent payments.

Most of the bad managers I've had since Psycho Manager were ones that I inherited when I bought buildings, not ones that I hired myself. Hiring a good apartment manager is something of an art form, and it takes practice to learn which applicants for the job are trustworthy. Looks are deceiving; in fact, one of the best managers I ever had wasn't a handsome man at all. My favorite manager wasn't someone that people would describe as "fit" or "trim". Quite the opposite; he was almost large enough to blot out the sun. He was an older gentleman as well. I never formally asked his age, but my best estimates put him in his early sixties.

Now, taking one glance into this man's home would have convinced you that he was a terrible property manager. He lived in absolute filth. It wasn't the sort of rotten-food-and-swarms-of-bugs filth that requires calling in a hazmat team, but nothing in his dwelling was ever in its rightful place either. He was a complete slob. His lack of cleanliness wasn't even the most surprising thing about him – the first time I visited him at home, I was surprised to find a cute little Asian girl tending to him as he slumped in his chair. She was young enough to be his daughter – she was no more than twenty years old – but I soon found out she was a mail-order bride he'd purchased from China to be his wife. I'd never actually seen a mail-order bride before, and I was shocked; I couldn't get over the sight of this girl showing such devotion and loyalty to a husband three times her age.

Mr. Mail Order Bride wasn't the only eccentric manager I ever came across, either. Another favorite of mine was a middle-aged woman who kept a veritable flock of children in her own apartment. It was as if she lived in the middle of the primate enclosure at a zoo; young children were everywhere, climbing furniture, screaming, throwing valuables around, jumping on beds and running up and down hallways. Fortunately, her chaotic home life was no reflection of her work style. She had the building running like clockwork; rent was collected on time, and she provided a good model for the other tenants.

Most of the managers you'll encounter in your career, however, aren't exceptional in any way. They're not drug lords or criminal masterminds, nor are they shining examples of efficiency and foresight. It's laziness that runs rampant in the property management world. Most managers you'll meet don't like to work, collect rent, schedule maintenance, pick up garbage or talk to tenants. They'd prefer to sit in their offices playing solitaire and getting paid for having a pulse. There's only so much you can do with an apartment manager like that. A stern talking-to may help temporarily, or it may drive the disgruntled manager to fill the units with neo-Nazis who burn effigies of you on the lawn. Most of the time, it's best to send a bad manager packing and start again with a new one.

There are a wide range of property managers out there, of every shape, size and capability. If you're planning on staying in the real estate business for a long time, you'll run across them all – the good, the bad and the ugly. Some of them will enrich your business and come up with great ideas you'd never have dreamed of. Some will make you wish you'd chosen another career entirely. Perseverance is key – there are a lot of people in the business, and there are plenty of hardworking managers ready to be hired. Now, go find them!

CHAPTER NINE

Inspections or I Would Rather Have a Tooth Pulled with No Shots

Inspections are just a part of life. You wouldn't buy a horse without checking its teeth. You wouldn't purchase fruit without looking it over for some new species of extra-deadly fungal growth. Likewise, the first thing to do before buying a new building is to go in there and see what you can see.

Nine times out ten when you enter a tenant's unit, you're going to find nothing out of the ordinary. They'll be perfectly nice people with tidy apartments, clean floors, lovely children and all of their BDSM fetish gear properly tucked away in the cupboard where it belongs. You can safely poke around the unit and continue on your merry way, without any notable psychological trauma sustained.

It's that tenth tenant you need to worry about.

There's no telling what you'll find when you swing open the door of a unit. There could be drugs. There could be prostitution. Angry dogs. Polygamy. Genetically engineered dog-sized cockroaches. Alligators. Clowns. The list is endless. It takes a lot, then, to really stand out as an exceptionally bad tenant; a person has to go to considerable effort if they want to be remembered from the hundreds of vagrants and junkies I've encountered over the decades.

Two of my favorite tenants lived in a 104-unit building in Phoenix that my brother and I had endeavored to buy with three elderly Jewish men from Chicago. Because I was the only one foolish enough to willingly live in the desert wasteland of Arizona (dry heat, Yea Right), the task of inspecting the place fell on me. The building was a fine, upstanding place with boarded-up windows and missing doors, and it was inhabited by the sorts of fine, upstanding people who enjoy broken glass and plywood in their interior décor. Several people had kindly taken the liberty of house-sitting the vacant units for us, free of charge, and a few industrious entrepreneurs had even started their own amateur brothels and pharmacies in other vacant units. Sadly, because we were planning to renovate the building and return it to acceptable human living standards, I had to inform the members of this industrious little community that they would need to find a new building that suited their refined tastes.

Let me interrupt my own fascinating story to give a little advice to all those readers who aspire to one day clear vagrants out of rundown buildings of their very own. Before you take it upon yourself to employ some well-muscled meathead to help you clear the building, you should look into hiring someone uncomfortably close to your very nose – one of the vagrants you're trying to clear. For the price of a sandwich or a particularly fancy coffee, he'll do a much better job keeping people away than any rent-a-cop could even dream of.

Now, by this point, most of the residents sleeping in the building were under an agreement that paying rent just wasn't necessary for them. A few, however, were still living under the unpopular "paying money in exchange for living somewhere" system, and it was two of these paying tenants that really stick out in my mind.

The first one appeared to be paying his rent by selling the sorts of substances that star in their own soft-focus Public Service Announcements. I would love to elaborate more on him here, but drug dealers are such rich, colorful characters that it seems wrong to lump them in with the other empty shells of human beings that one routinely comes across in distressed buildings.

The second tenant, however, didn't have any drugs coming out of her apartment. In fact, it looked like nothing ever left her apartment in any form – not food, not garbage, and not even the aggressive mold taking up residence on every available surface of her home. The proud owner of these mounds of worthless junk was a little old lady who was all by herself, and was not shy about telling me that she was keeping it that way. My request to inspect her unit was met with reasonable hesitation, followed by slightly less reasonable screaming and yelling. The woman weighed less than a wet Golden Retriever, but she was quite insistent that I was not getting into her apartment.

There's a rule of building ownership in Arizona that goes something like this: if you give the tenant 48 hours notice, you can do whatever you want. You can go in and inspect their units, you can install a lava lamp in every room of the apartment, you can host a community Riverdance tournament in the living room – anything goes. I stapled a notice to the door of this geriatric hoarder's home, and I informed the very nice men at the City of Phoenix Police Department that I might possibly need their help getting past a stubborn octogenarian to inspect her home.

Two days went past, and I rallied the maintenance man, manager and two police officers, and we went to pay my stubborn resident a visit. Of course, when she poked her head out and saw the group of large, burly men bearing down on her, she immediately relented, inviting us in for a warm plate of cookies and a nice cup of tea.

Oh, no, wait; she didn't do that at all. Instead, she walked right out of her unit and sucker-punched me straight in the face.

The police immediately detained the Rock 'Em Sock 'Em grandma, and explained to her that civilized people don't go about punching their building owners in the face like that. I declined to press charges against her; her wrinkly little fist had surprised me, but she hadn't actually managed to cause any injury. With her safely lapsing into hysterics in the policemen's arms, I braved the journey into her apartment.

Three seconds into my inspection, it became painfully apparent that the woman hadn't thrown anything away since the downfall of Yugoslavia – the place was filled with rotting food, decaying magazines, assorted garbage, and the types of corny knick-knacks that become mandatory for women as soon as they collect their first senior's discount. The only thing in her apartment that still worked as intended was the floor, and even that was currently playing host to a frolicking, lively colony of green molds. Dealing with this woman would have been a task more suited to a sturdy psychiatrist or a trashy lifestyle reality show, but since I'd bought the building housing her unwashed disaster zone, it was my responsibility to deal with her. And deal with her I did. Just like any other elderly hoarder and Jewish property management pair, we became fast friends; over the next few weeks, I was even able to help her clean the place out and turn it from "serious biohazard" to "normal, livable apartment".

That little old lady wasn't the worst hoarder I'd ever encounter – not by a long shot. She may have had her fair share of knickknacks and garbage, but even if she'd put real effort into collecting useless goods, she could never have even aspired to what I found in another apartment. I've seen Greek art in apartments before, but I never expected to come across a full-blown labyrinth from Greek lore. The proud owners of this maze were a couple of hoarders, who constructed their 800 square foot masterpiece out of old newspapers and magazines. The pages stacked from floor to ceiling – only narrow hallways snaking between useful parts of the unit were clear. It was like a wondrous childhood corn maze, except that it was horribly unsafe and in direct violation of health codes.

Unfortunately, not all of my tenant inspection stories are so innocent.

In my second year as a property manager, I managed an apartment building near the Arizona State University campus. It wasn't a student housing building; puking college students and occasional farm animal-based pranks, I could have handled. This was a regular old apartment building in rough shape. The owner of the building suspected that he had some less-than-legal chemical and plant substances coming in and out of the building, and he called me in for an inspection. I promptly stuck up the usual '48 hours' notice that says I can do whatever I want in here notifications, and two days later, I met the building manager.

While the owner may have had a drug problem, the manager looked like she, in fact, had a drug hobby. Her complexion belonged on a B-movie monster. She looked to be in her late 30's or early 40's, but I was certain she hadn't slept since she was old enough to drive a car. She was tiny, which wasn't necessarily her fault, and she was a smoker, which was certainly her fault. Regardless, I tried to be nice. She told me that a whopping six units out of the sixteen total were vacant, so I asked to see those empty apartments first.

Now, I know what an empty apartment looks like. I have seen many of them. What I've never seen is an empty apartment that has food in the fridge, dirty dishes in the sinks, clothes in the closets, bedding on the floor and still-smoldering cigarettes on the counter. Those six apartments were either occupied by hungry, smoking ghosts, or there was something sinister going on at this building.

There may not have been paranormal creatures in the vacant apartments, but the people in the occupied ones weren't far from it. They hovered over my shoulders like not-so-friendly ghosts, watching my every movement in their apartments. Half of the people I saw in there may have very well had one foot in the grave, having clearly mixed up their daily vitamins with very different kinds of pills. I'd seen enough, and I figured that the person most interested in hearing my findings would be the watchful, responsible property manager.

To say that I was a little bit mistaken would be like saying cinder-blocks are a little bit inedible.

I reported the results of my inspection through her screen door, and the skinny, run-down greyhound of a manager became a snapping, snarling pit bull in a heartbeat. I hadn't thought that a human being could throw such a fit without first contracting late-stage rabies. She proceeded to threaten me, my coworkers, my family, my friends, my dentist, my fourth-grade teacher, my mail carrier, and everyone else I had ever met. She wanted me off the property, off the job, and out of her business. Being threatened by a deranged human being is one of those things that always sounds terrifying on paper, but as it was, having an anemic woman pounding her tiny fists on a screen door at me was about as terrifying as being growled at by a Chihuahua stuffed in a woman's purse.

The manager and I quickly realized that our snarling pit bull was the alpha dog in a pack of drug dealers, running their very own drug ring in the apartment building. Those so-called 'vacant units' weren't vacant at all – I'm not stupid or believe in paranormal activity– but rather the homes of drug-dealing tenants whose rent payments went directly into the manager's pocket. Needless to say, the owner wasn't exactly bouncing up and down with glee when he found out he was unknowingly playing host to his very own episode of *Breaking Bad,* and quickly put the muzzle on his crooked manager.

Cleaning up this sorry dog pound fell onto my shoulders. I chose to hire off-duty police officers to secure the place at night, instead of security company staff. I had two reasons for doing this:

1. It sounds a whole lot cooler.

2. The police are actually capable of making arrests.

I later came to find out that the property dissolved into actual gun-fights between the police and residents when the sun went down, like some kind of bizarre, drug-fuelled werewolf tale, but a few weeks of arrests and gunshots had most of the unsavories cleared out.

While we're on the topic of dogs, there's a rule in property man-agement that says your dog has to be put away when the place is inspected. I have no way of knowing if Mr. Cuddles is a fuzzy bundle of love or a ruthless guard animal, and I frankly don't have much interest in finding out. During one inspection of a small apartment building, however, one resident forgot. We tried to inspect her apartment and came face-to-face with her enormous, panting German Shepherd. It might have been snarling and growl-ing to entice us to play with it, but decided to run away from it just in case we were mistaken.

As luck would have it, the owner of that charming animal was nowhere to be found; the closest person we could find was her ine-briated next-door neighbor, who assured us that it was a very nice doggie and that it would never bite us. The property manager I was with decided that it would be an excellent idea to usher the poor drunk woman into the apartment to soothe the savage beast. Since

I consider myself to be a human being with at least an ounce of sense, I immediately recognized this as a terrible idea on multiple levels.

Of course, he didn't listen.

He was egging this woman on like a young schoolboy chanting for a classmate to touch his tongue to a frozen metal pole; eventually, it did the trick. Our drunken new friend went barreling into the apartment. On its part, the dog reacted just as any reasonable person reacts when an inebriated stranger comes hurtling towards him in his own home; he opened his jaws wide and chomped them down on her leg.

There really weren't enough "I told you so's" for that moment. The woman was reacting just as any intoxicated individual who has been bitten by a strange dog usually reacts – she was screaming and shouting and crying. Luckily, the dog hadn't broken the skin, which spared me from having a second funny story to tell about a trip to the emergency room. I locked up the dog-guarded apartment, and we all learned a valuable lesson about listening to me when I say something is a terrible idea.

My encounters with interesting critters doesn't stop with dogs. By the end of my property management career, I'd seen just about everything including hamsters, fish, snails, chinchillas, ferrets, lizards, and tarantulas; they all fail to impress me. But one animal that did make an impression on me was a rather large snake.

I was inspecting a unit just a few doors down from the magazine hoarders I mentioned. The apartment belonged to some American

Indians, and it was relatively clean, quiet, and free of deadly reptiles. I was just about to move on to the next unit when a strange man came in – whether he was a friend, family member, or total stranger to the residents, I'll never know. Whatever his relationship to the people in the apartment, he'd decided to gift them with a large, menacing snake that he'd seen no reason to safely confine to any kind of container.

Now, snakes don't bother me too much. Most people might consider it rude to barge into a house unannounced with a snake in tow, but the particular tribe that my American Indian residents belonged to considered it nothing less than a bad omen, ushering in injury, disease, death, crop failure, poor marriages, noisy children, sick houseplants, cold tea, warm beer and itches in hard-to-reach places. In fact, they considered the presence of the scaly serpent such bad luck that they were ready to pack up and move out of the apartment right then and there. That day, I went from property manager to amateur therapist as I calmed down the tenants and convinced them not to abandon their home for the sake of an uninvited houseguest.

I never did find out why the man had brought them the snake.

Yes, over the years I've seen it all – garbage, lunatics, hobos, reptiles, large mammals, entire libraries, drug rings, and more cockroaches than I will ever care to remember. I'll give my tenants credit where credit is due; most of them are sane, tidy people, living in clean, tidy apartments. And despite how crazy I might seem by this point in the book, I go into every apartment I inspect desperately hoping that I won't find an apocalyptic-scale mess inside.

But luck isn't always on my side, and every so often, I come across the kind of apartment that makes me call for a hazmat team and a good therapist. Dealing with these sorts of places is expensive, time-consuming, and some effort. In the end, though, it's okay. Because if nothing else, it makes for a great story.

CHAPTER TEN

My Second Date with Phoenix SWAT

Now, by this point in the book, you might be convinced that I'm some sort of property-managing lunatic, precariously teetering on the border between stable, functioning member of society and dangerous madman eating the laces off of his own straightjacket. As you may recall, despite my fascination with managing murderers, garbage hoarders, and drug dealers, I managed to catch the eye of the Phoenix SWAT team. They must have taken a liking to me, because I was lucky enough to get a second date with them. Of course, I said yes. Who wouldn't? The men on the SWAT team are courageous, dedicated, and steadfast in the face of danger.

Oh, and they also carry really nice guns.

Neither one of my dates with the SWAT team took place during my time as a manager – the team must be especially fond of retail brokers, because the second encounter with them happened while I was in the midst of selling off a property I would one day come to partially own.

It all started on another sunny, sweltering day in hot, sticky Phoenix. Nothing was out of the ordinary – the birds were singing, the squirrels were scurrying, and unattended full-grown pit bulls wandered about, chewing on the remains of what looked horribly like birds and squirrels. You see, I was representing a buyer in the purchase of two four-plexes in a wonderful, family-friendly south Phoenix neighborhood; family friendly provided that your family derived some or all of its income from participating in a variety of illegal activity.

Now, before the buyer was to shell out his hard-earned money for the property, a physical inspection had to be done. As you might recall from the last chapter I needed to go into each unit and look around for broken pipes, crumbling plaster, faulty wiring, vengeful ghosts, and anything else that might decrease the value of the property. Easy, right?

Did I mention that the buildings were inhabited by a notorious drug gang?

And when I say that they were inhabited by a drug gang, I don't mean that one or two of the units housed gang members. Every single one of the eight units on the property was being rented by someone with a connection to the gang. Best of all, the gang's leader – a young man named Jamal – was in residence, and we were assured that he wouldn't be pleased about two middle-aged men poking around his home.

I knew Jamal was a delightful character, before I even met him. He was an industrious fellow; in addition to his primary, drug-related career, he ran a hobby business in his home, breeding and raising vicious pit bull dogs. He wasn't a very big man – he stood perhaps five feet, six inches and probably weighed in at around 130lbs – but the .357 magnum he kept perpetually strapped to his hip ensured that no one underestimated him for his size.

Being shot by an angry drug dealer wasn't exactly high on my "to-do" list, and so it was decided that a police escort would accompany us on our inspection. My client and I were about as fond of drug gangs as we were of being mauled by dogs, so we secured an animal control unit to assist with the inspection as well. This wouldn't be a routine inspection, but it didn't have to be difficult either – with the dogs cleared out and a few uniformed cops along, we figured that this inspection didn't have to be a big production.

You can imagine our surprise when we arrived at the property to find a SWAT team.

We'd scheduled the inspection for eight or nine in the morning, and when the buyer and I showed up, we were greeted by eight members of the Phoenix SWAT team. They weren't in the full riot gear that they usually wear in the movies, but the semi-automatic weapons they carried meant they were well-protected. There were four of us there to do the inspection – me, my assistant, the buyer, and an inspector – and we were told to wait on the street while the SWAT team made the building safe for us.

Now, I don't want you to read this and think that encountering the SWAT team is a bi-weekly occurrence in the property management business. To come across them once in your entire career is rare. To come across them twice in such a short span of time was probably a clear sign that I needed to start dealing with properties in nicer areas of town.

While we were waiting on the sidewalk, the entire group of SWAT members decided to drop by and see how Jamal was doing. He opened the door, pistol on hip as always, to find the barrels of eight guns pointed at him. With nowhere to run or hide, Jamal proceeded to demonstrate a shocking lack of self-preservation by yelling and threatening the very men pointing guns at his head. When he'd finally realized that this was not a battle he had any chance of winning, Jamal and his family were led out to the building's court-yard and surrounded by four of the SWAT members; there were no fewer than four guns pointed at him for the rest of the inspection.

With Jamal himself out of the way, it was time to deal with his pre-cious pets. Animal control had sent us along with not one, but two trucks; we had enough equipment there to round up a family of bears. The animal control officers used loops of rope on the ends of long sticks – they looked like sad, modern versions of the lasso – and brought out not two, not three, but four snapping and snarl-ing pit bulls. The dogs had evidently had plenty of spare time in between guarding their drug-dealing master, as six puppies were also taken from the house. I'm ordinarily fine with friendly dogs, but I didn't think that a gangster's guard dogs were too eager to jump up and lick my face. When the dogs were safely loaded into the animal control trucks, the SWAT teams continued clearing the building.

The SWAT team then started on the rest of the building. It was the same at every unit – there was a knock on the door, the occupant opened up to find himself with a face full of guns, and the family was led into the courtyard to spend some quality bonding time with Jamal at gunpoint. Finally, we were ready to start inspecting.

Jamal was not at all happy about this impromptu evacuation, or the impending home inspections, and he wasn't shy about voicing his opinions. As we walked past him on our way to the first apartment, he threatened to murder everyone from our spouses to our future grandchildren's coworkers, and everyone in between. We calmly informed him that he'd have to join the long line of other miscreants who'd threatened our lives countless times before, and started to look through the house.

Structurally, the buildings were fine. Everything turned on and off as it should, nothing leaked or sparked and nothing was obviously decaying in front of our very eyes. Even more surprising, there was no sign that these units belonged to hardened criminals – there was no drug paraphernalia, murder weapons or live hostages to be seen. Everything seemed to be neat and orderly.

At least, until we found the hole.

There are plenty of places in a house – namely on the walls and doors – that a person might reasonably expect to find a little hole here or here. Walls get kicked or punched in fits of drunkenness and rage. Children and adults throw things or drop things. Large pets don't always know their own strength. Ceilings are another story. Unless you have a giant for a roommate, most people aren't even capable of reaching the ceiling, never mind punching through it. Making a hole in your ceiling requires either exceptionally bad aim or deliberate malicious intent. In this case, it seemed to be a bit of both.

The hole in the ceiling of one of the units was huge, and suspiciously man-shaped. I'd never expected to see anything quite like it outside of a "Looney Tunes" cartoon, and we called in the SWAT team to see if they found it as interesting as we did. We were promptly ushered out of the apartment while the SWAT time rummaged about in the broken ceiling, and they eventually emerged with an entire trash bag full of marijuana. Not a baggie. Not a brick. An entire, standard-sized garbage bag that a saner person might fill with yard clippings or lots of old clothes. It appeared that one of the tenants was storing drugs in his ceiling, and had taken a shortcut back to his apartment through the ceiling one day while retrieving some. We didn't stick around that unit long enough to find out if anyone was ever arrested for it.

After the ceiling incident, the rest of the inspection was a breeze. Jamal even seemed less murderous when we passed him by on our way out; the SWAT team had served food to their captive audience, and it's tough to make a menacing threat when you're chowing down on pizza in your yard.

After all that fuss, my buyer did end up purchasing the building. He gave it some much-needed rehabilitation, drove the drug gang out, and even acquired some of the neighboring lots. I eventually sold it off again in 2009. Jamal and his buddies were spotted in the area, but they appeared to be doing little more than a sightseeing tour of their old homes – they never caused us any trouble again.

Two run-ins with the SWAT team was more than I could have hoped for, and I'm still waiting on that third date to this day. I did, however, hear of another SWAT operation through a colleague. My associate was listing an enormous building – the ink had barely dried on the print ads – when it was raided in the largest SWAT drug bust in Phoenix history. That's the sort of news that you might want delivered in person, or by telephone, but my colleague had no such luck; he found out the exact same time the rest of the city did, when it was splattered across the newspaper headlines the next day. The building was massive, with somewhere near 120 residents, located in a questionable part of town. In the raid, 60 people – half of the building's population – were arrested. Even the manager was in on it.

What made this SWAT raid interesting, besides its sheer scale, was how clueless the owner was. I gave up name-calling in the second grade, but the woman's skull would have been better off being put to use as a punch bowl instead of a brain casing. Even though the owner actually occupied one of the units in the building, she was completely blindsided when the raid took place. She wasn't a full-time resident, and members of her live-in drug ring simply ceased their drug activity when she popped by to use her apartment as office space. When she left again, it was business as usual.

Now, I'd like to tell you that dealing with these kinds of unsavory people is just a part of starting out in property management. I could claim that, twenty or thirty years into your career, you'll be dealing with nothing less than exquisite penthouses and fielding maintenance requests from celebrities. I think you already know I'd be lying to you. Just yesterday, the day before I sat down to write this, I was doing an inspection of a high-end complex in a nice part of town, when I was warned that one of the units went above and beyond the reasonable limits of disgusting. We had a crew of exterminators along with us, and those men are usually equipped to deal with anything. When you've spend a significant amount of your adult life picking up cockroach carcasses, there's just not a whole lot that can phase you anymore.

Apparently, this unit could. My bug guys were in there no more than five minutes, clutching their mouths in the universal "I'm about to projectile vomit onto the nearest slow-moving target" sign. Naturally, since it was too vile for people whose jobs are disgusting by nature, I decided I could handle it.

It wasn't a pretty sight. There was rotting food on every surface, water where there was no business being water, a thriving ecosystem of insects, and two young children who'd apparently been sentenced to wear the same dirty diapers until they got old enough to change themselves. No amount of air freshener could have salvaged the place. The tenant, who held on to a respectable career as a prostitute, barred us entry from one particular room, so, naturally, we went in anyways to find a man sprawled on the floor in a drugged stupor. As it turned out, she'd converted her living room into a literal "drug den". I wasn't shocked to find out that the tenants on either side of the unit had long ago moved out.

Luckily, the drugged-up prostitute tenant hadn't managed to do any lasting damage to the unit. We mentioned to the seller that we would prefer this delightful lady find other accommodations before we bought the building, and we went on our way. With any luck, the unit will be scrubbed, swabbed and fumigated by the time we're ready to take in a new tenant. Coming across tenants like these is sad – especially when young children are involved – but there's only so much you can do. Try to rent to tenants who aren't obviously criminals, psychopaths, or cleverly disguised dinosaurs, and deal with the poor tenants as they come.

Every time I deal with a rotting, foul unit, I dash out to my car and douse myself in hand sanitizer until I stop feeling like a human swamp creature. A place like the one I saw yesterday is enough to seriously deplete my reserves. Now that I think about it, while I'm out, I should pick out a new shirt. Maybe some clean underwear. Perhaps a smart new cologne.

Because I never know when the SWAT may come by for our third date.

CHAPTER ELEVEN

I Loved Property Management So Much That I Went Into Sales

I've revealed a lot about myself through the course of this book, but there's one very important fact that I haven't yet disclosed:

I hate property management.

As it turns out, devoting your time, money, energy, and life to something does not guarantee that you'll actually enjoy doing it, and with property management, I had to learn the hard way. My time as a property manager was long and fragmented. I mentioned earlier in the book that I started out in the property business in the early 1990's, buying and managing buildings. I purchased my first building the year the Backstreet Boys were formed, and by the time their third album came out, I'd sold off all my buildings and left the property game. I had made up my mind to forgo my worldly possessions and eke out a humble living in the wilderness.

Actually, I'd gotten a lucrative offer to return to the wine business and assist with the opening of a new winery. I took it.

After September 11, 2001, a winery job that involved frequent air travel was no longer as appealing as it had once been – especially with a young daughter at home. My brother had grown tired of living in a reasonable climate and decided to move to Arizona; together, we decided to start up our own Property Management business. It was perfect. Everyone loves a family business venture, and we knew what we were doing. It was guaranteed to be a success that would span the rest of our careers. And it was.

At least, it was until I quit in 2003.

I had several big reasons for quitting. As you may have suspected, hating property management may have been a large part of it. The other large part of it had to do with the complications of running a business with a blood relative – it's tough to maintain a professional relationship with someone who has been free to refer to you as an "asshole" for their entire adult life. My brother and I weren't ordinary siblings either; we have a thirteen-year age gap between us. We didn't grow up together. I was leaving home as he was starting kindergarten, and it's tough for a teenage boy to relate to his finger painting kid brother. Working together as business partners was the first chance we ever got to catch up on thirteen years of missed sibling rivalry, and the results weren't always good for our clients.

It wasn't just family dynamics and passionate hatred that drove me from property management either – money played a role. There wasn't enough money or enough work for two people at the head of our property management business, and since money was my entire reason for going into property management, that wasn't something I could overlook. I figured that selling buildings might be more lucrative than yelling at drug dealers who live in buildings, and as it turned out, I was right.

I started looking around for a new workplace. There's an old adage about large fish and small bodies of water, and so I decided to dip my toe into real estate brokerage at a small, friendly group. I didn't actually receive any broker training – that would have made everything far too easy – so they threw me into a little office and let me figure out how to swim for myself.

If you ever find yourself trying to succeed as a real estate broker with absolutely no training, don't panic. There are only two things you need to do: work hard, and provide good service to your clients. That's it. That's all you need to know. If you can do those two things consistently, not only will you succeed as a broker, you'll be one of the best brokers your clients will ever deal with.

I started off small with a very big client. I was sitting in my glorified broom closet of an office when a man-shaped mountain strolled in, looking to sell off some property. He was from Sin City and he drove what appeared to be a municipal garbage dump on wheels, but he was one of the nicest men I've ever met. This man was the not-so-proud owner of ten, four-plexes that he'd purchased together as a forty-unit property. He wanted to sell the units as he'd bought them – in one piece. I disagreed. I told the man that he'd make far more money selling them separately, and though he disagreed, he decided to trust me.

Now, keep in mind that I was new. I had no experience. No one would put a new driver behind the wheel of a half-million dollar race car. No one would put a recent high school graduate at the helm of a corporation. No one scours the Yellow Pages for untested electricians to hire. And yet, with his property's profit at stake, this man decided to trust me.

I then became the first person to ever hand him a cheque for one million dollars. He promptly lost it all in Vegas, but I was a little wiser with my commission.

After that, I worked my way up from a property pauper to the full-on King of Four-Plexes. A four-plex is not a popular building for brokers; they're tiny residential buildings, and most people in real estate would prefer to sell sprawling, multi-million-dollar skyscrapers with built-in restaurants and opera theatres. The humble four-plex became my domain. Small, residential properties like those were passed from broker to broker like a game of real estate "hot potato" before they finally landed on my desk. Four-plexes piled up on my desk – in groups of five, ten, twenty, thirty or forty – and I sold them one-by-one, turning an incredible profit.

So what made the individual four-plex such a success? It was simple, really. When I was starting my broker career, the economy was hot and everyone wanted a piece of the lucrative real estate market. It was a numbers game – there are far more small-time buyers looking for a first building than there are real estate moguls looking to buy up half a city block. And since these were residential buildings, most of them qualified for residential funding. In those days, the funding was easy to get – so long as you didn't live under a stained mattress in an alleyway, you could probably qualify.

Then, of course, there were negative equity loans. The premise of them was fantastic, provided you lived in a limitless utopia of endless growth. Your payments for the property were low and the equity of the buildings was slowly bled away, but property values were appreciating so quickly that none of that mattered. All you had to do was buy a property on a negative equity loan, hold on to it for a while, and then sell it at a sky-high profit. You couldn't lose – unless, of course, you happened to still be holding onto a negative equity loan when the bottom fell out of the economy in 2008. Investors who had sold off their holdings by 2007 are probably taking baths in their money right now. Investors who still had negative equity loans to their name when the country collectively found out what a risk they were are probably heating up TV dinners over camp stoves right now. Real estate can be funny like that.

When the sub-prime mortgage crisis hit, I was right in the thick of it. It was the real estate equivalent of living in a Michael Bay action movie. Devastating? Yes. Explosive? Of course. A lot of fun? Obviously. The banks themselves had been sitting on the financial equivalent of quicksand – many banks had purchased ten or twenty individual properties all at once with a single, multi-million-dollar sub-prime loan, and when the crisis hit, they started to sink fast. These negative equity loans weren't your garden-variety loans that could be paid off bit by bit; you either forked over the amount in full, or you started filling out bankruptcy forms. An individual declaring bankruptcy isn't exactly reason to throw a picnic, but if personal bankruptcy is a rainstorm, a bank defaulting is a full-fledged hurricane.

If the banks were going to pay off their twenty-property loans, they would have to sell off all twenty properties at once – that was where I came in, closing all those deals in a single day. Selling two dozen properties at once is not a small undertaking. At the height of the crisis, I was more of a rock star than a Realtor®, pitching properties in front of crowds of hundreds of prospective buyers. I even became notable enough in my company to star in my own television commercial.

Most of the four-plexes I dealt with were functioning, livable apartments, but every so often, I'd be tasked with selling one that was little more than four-part urban shanty. They weren't just in need of a little tender love and care – some of them had no electricity. Or running water. Or air conditioning. Or windows.

You get the point.

Old, broken houses aren't the only things I deal with that have a little "character". Anyone who has ever dealt with customers will tell you – in between screaming fits – that it can be trying. My real estate buyers were no different, especially because I dealt with dozens of people new to the business. Now, I can understand missing a few details. I don't expect new buyers to spot roof damage from a mile away or detect termites by finely-tuned instinct alone. What I do expect buyers to do is understand basic loan procedures.

Banks don't intentionally shroud their loan procedures in foggy, bureaucratic mystery. Why would they? They want your loan to go through quickly, so they can start to collect their sweet, sweet interest from it. A child borrowing money to start a lemonade stand could understand the process. Your suitability for a loan is determined by your debt-to-income ratio. If you're a frugal aero-space engineer, you're probably all set for that loan. If you owe your first-born child to creditors, you may need to turn to black-market organ sales to earn the money instead. Now, a loan isn't an "event", but a process. And if you do something to significantly alter your income-to-debt ratio during that process – like, for instance, if you quit your job, or begin construction on a private menagerie in your backyard – the entire loan has to be scrapped and the pro-cess has to be re-started. This seems like a simple concept, but I had an alarming number of my clients who couldn't seem to grasp it. They'd purchase a yacht on credit on their way home from the bank, and be genuinely surprised when they were told they'd need to re-submit their loan paperwork.

It's not always the buyer who's the source of intrigue, either. Sellers can be just as strange. On multiple occasions, I've had sellers sim-ply disappear. Their building doesn't go anywhere, but out of the blue, the seller himself is nowhere to be found. I don't know if they skipped town or been swallowed by the mighty jaws of a great white shark. They could be lounging on a beach or caught up in an international espionage mission in another country. All I know is that they aren't signing sale papers.

My favorite mishap, though, is the time I got sued. It started out as a little issue with a little bug – the bed bug, to be exact. Children across the country are tucked into bed with instructions to not "let the bed bugs bite", but at this building, they were apparently biting. When I was sold the building, I had no idea that the place was host to the bed-dwelling creepy-crawlies, but not long after the deal was sealed, tenants started coming forward with complaints. The buyer naturally decided that my inability to telepathically detect bedbug infestations made the entire mess my fault, and sued me. Then the seller realized that I must have intentionally released a horde of bed bugs into his building, and joined in the lawsuit frenzy. The tenants who'd actually been bitten by the insects smelled money and threw their hats into the legal ring. By the time the dust cleared, my commission on that building had been eaten up by damage payouts and I was ready to put the entire mess behind me.

Despite the messes, mortgage crises and lawsuits, I continue to sell small buildings. There's where the money is and that's where my heart lies. I'm not half-bad at it either, or I wouldn't be sitting here writing this book. Property management was how I got my start, and where I got most of my stories, but ultimately it was brokerage that won the day, and gave me a whole other set of stories to tell. Will my real estate broker days ever warrant their own book? Maybe. Maybe not. It's been a long time since I put management behind me, and I'm gathering more material by the day.

But ultimately, this book isn't about me. Sure, it's filled with my stories, and it's got my name on the cover, but it's not about me. It's about you, hypothetical aspiring property manager or real estate investor, who picked up this book. My stories have been shared amongst my family and friends so many times that they're all incredibly sick of them by now, but I recorded them here so that you could take my advice and learn from my mistakes. In the end, it doesn't even matter if this book inspired you to press on with your property management career, or drove you to run screaming into a different vocation.

I just hope you had a good laugh along the way.

ABOUT THE AUTHOR

Terry Kass is a licensed Broker and expert in the Phoenix, AZ real estate market. Consistently a top sales performer, Terry has owned, managed, and sold apartments in the Phoenix market since 1993. He holds the prestigous designations of CCIM (Certified Commercial Investment Member) and CPM (Certified Property Manager), and is skilled in delivering tailored real estate solutions for his clients.

His company, GPCI AZ, LLC provides management, brokerage, research, due diligence, market and feasibility study, and valuation services to apartment investors. Terry's success can be attributed to his exceptional analytical and sound decision-making abilities. GPCI serves a diverse group of individuals from around the country who own apartments in the Phoenix market.

In addition to his exceptional knowledge of the apartment real estate market, Terry is a nationally known wine industry expert with over 25 years experience representing wineries from all over the world.

Terry's track record of success in different industries enables him to share intimate knowledge on a variety of subjects including marketing, management, and sales.

REACH TERRY AT:

Terry@GPCI-AZ.com

www.GPCI-AZ.com